ADAPTING ARCHITECTURAL DETAILS
for Quilts

ADAPTING ARCHITECTURAL DETAILS
for Quilts

CAROL WAGNER

PHOTOGRAPHY BY HOWARD & CAROL WAGNER

American Quilter's Society

P.O. BOX 3290, PADUCAH, KY 42002

Library of Congress Cataloging-in-Publication Data

Wagner, Carol.
Adapting architectural details for quilts/Carol Wagner; photography by Howard & Carol Wagner.
p. cm.
ISBN 0-89145-976-6: $12.95
1. Patchwork – Patterns. 2. Architecture in art. I. Title.
TT835.W33 1992   746.46'041 – dc20   91-46031

Additional copies of this book may be ordered from:

American Quilter's Society
P.O. Box 3290
Paducah, KY 42002-3290

@$12.95 Add $1.00 for postage & handling.

Printed by IMAGE GRAPHICS, INC., Paducah, Kentucky

Dedication

TO HOWARD

for all of his encouragement and patience during the months I worked on this book.

Acknowledgments

Several people deserve an extra **thank you** for their help:

my husband, Howard,
> for help with the photography and the quick course
> on using a word processor;

Lori Olsson, Anita Murphy, and Jeanne Tanamachi
> for their exquisite hand quilting;

Violette Jahnke
> for taking time to shoot some special photos;

Runyon's management;
> and the

Cathedral of St. Paul, & St. Luke's Catholic Church.

Table of Contents

SECTION I

ARCHITECTURE
AS
INSPIRATION

CHAPTER 1   *Locating Decorative Architecture*

CHAPTER 2   *Architectural Photography & Resources*

1
CHAPTER

LOCATING DECORATIVE ARCHITECTURE

As we go about our daily routines of going to work or doing errands, most of us have become very oblivious to our surroundings. We drive on the same streets, ride on the same buses and walk on the same sidewalks day after day. Our senses have become so dulled by the familiarity of our routes that we are not even aware of the unusual design sources that appear all around us. We do not realize that many of these designs could be adapted into patterns that can be used to make our quilts.

Exciting and unusual designs appear in the architecture all around us. These designs can be found on many of the older buildings that are scattered throughout our cities. Many of these structures are lavishly embellished with ornate carvings and gingerbread or decorative frieze designs on their facades. We walk through foyers, hallways or lobbies daily, ignoring the variety of patterns set in ceramic tile beneath our feet. With a bit of imagination, these architectural ornamentations can be adapted into unique, one-of-a-kind patterns for our quilts.

Buildings constructed between the mid-1800's and the early 1900's were embellished with great amounts of decoration. Italianate, Gothic Revival, Stick, and Queen Anne homes of the Victorian era nearly exploded with lavish gingerbread. Every surface was covered with elaborate fretwork, cast plaster moldings, scrolled bargeboards, terra cotta reliefs, carved woodwork, cast iron cresting, or stained glass.

Though the Art Deco movement of the early twentieth century was much less ornate, it had its own decorative styles. Its motifs were stylized with more flowing lines and featured a less cluttered design. It had a more modern look. Office buildings, banks and

stores constructed during this era usually had some form of decoration on their exterior surfaces. Churches were elaborately embellished with hand-carved wood panels and doors inside, and carved stone detailing outside. Public libraries, post office buildings, and courthouses were richly decorated with assorted design motifs. We need to take a fresh look around us, like tourists visiting our city for the first time, to become aware of the many pattern possibilities that architectural embellishments can offer.

These old buildings are scattered throughout our cities, and they are easy to spot. Their exteriors are often discolored by years of soot or water streaks. They are built out of brick or huge blocks of brownstone, limestone, or granite, and sometimes they are faced with marble. Some of these structures are quite large, covering half a city block, but usually they are not too tall, perhaps five to six stories. Occasionally they can be as high as 15 or 16 stories. Many of them are smaller stores or shops, only two to three stories high, and they may have elaborate designs around their windows and doors. Some of these small buildings have false fronts which make them appear taller. It is not uncommon for these buildings to have a car-

The Minneapolis saloon, shown above, is typical of small buildings constructed in the late 1880's. These structures are often well worth investigation. Inside this saloon I found a wonderful floor tile pattern that resembled a large quilt. As shown in the photos left and right, one section of the floor design became the inspiration for a small wallhanging, which I entitled TULIP STAR.

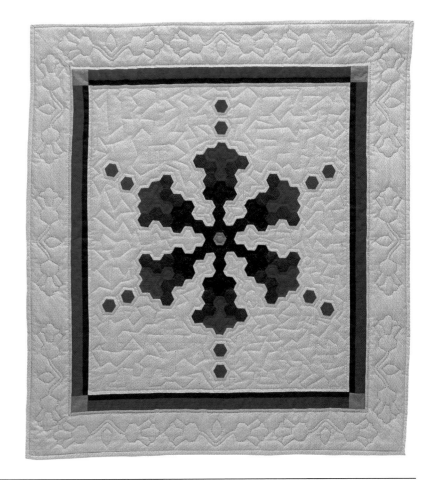

touche, or a scrolled emblem, bearing a name or date, or a decorative plaque set above the main entrance as well as some decorative stone or terra cotta trim around the window.

There have been many changes in our cities in the past few decades. There may not be much of this aged architecture remaining in the heart of a city's main business or retail section. Many of these fine old structures have been torn down because of urban renewal projects and commercial redevelopment. They have been replaced by taller buildings constructed of glass and steel, and some have been replaced by parking ramps and even expressways. Fortunately, urban redevelopment has bypassed some of these treasures. Even though they may have undergone facelifts and remodelling at the street level, up above, traces of the original structure can often still be seen, with some of the ornamental trim intact. If you walk a block or two away from the main downtown thoroughfares to the side streets, you may find several buildings, large or small, that still retain elaborate trimmings.

Older residential neighborhoods have some good examples of these old buildings, too. There can be a school or public library located on a side street that has some excellent exterior decoration. Churches found on quiet, tree-lined streets may have some marvelous designs on or around their doors that can inspire you. Homes built during the Victorian era are well known for excessive use of gingerbread embellishings.

When you spot an old building, stop and take a few moments to examine its surface for potential quilt patterns. Start with the entrance. Often there is some sort of carving or intricate design above the door. Is there anything there that could be adapted? Then let your eyes move up the exterior surface. Sometimes an ornate frieze of terra cotta encircles the walls of the building. Look above the windows for swags, crests, or shell patterns. Frequently some decorative trim can be found here too. Always look at the upper corners of the building to see if there are any corbels or brackets under the edges of the eaves. Quite often there are wonderfully elaborate embellishments located there such as graceful swirls, fierce gargoyles, or smiling cherubs. There may be one or even several rows of repetitive designs along the eaves and on the bargeboards edging the gables. Some of them may be quite simple, but some of them may provide inspiration for a future quilt project. Soon you will become more and more aware of the many design possibilities on the exteriors of these old buildings, and you will be consciously looking for them, trying to find designs and embellishments.

ABOVE, TOP TO BOTTOM: *The Lincoln County Courthouse, Merrill, Wisconsin, is an impressive Victorian building. National Register of Historic Places signs, such as the one I found in front of this courthouse, encourage visitors to go inside. As is usually the case, the trip inside proved to be well worth the effort. I discovered intricate tile designs throughout the main floor, one of which is shown above, with others on following pages.*

OPPOSITE PAGE: *This is the 18 foot rotunda floor centerpiece I discovered as I looked down from the edge of the balcony. The photo above shows a section of the border design around this rotunda centerpiece. This one floor alone could inspire countless quilts!*

When you see an old public building or an old office building, go inside to see if there is any interior ornamentation in the lobby or foyer area. If there is an elevator, examine its outer doors and the walls on either side of it. There may be some intricate metalwork designs. Ceilings were not forgotten by yesterday's architect. His plans may have incorporated an embossed metal or cast plaster ceiling with plaster moldings along the edges. Take a good look at these interiors. Your next quilt pattern could be there.

Occasionally locating interior architectural designs may take a little detective work. However, there are clues that can indicate that something special can be hiding behind a closed door. One day, as I was walking past a building on a downtown side street, I noticed a ceramic tile design just outside the entrance. It was a clue to do some further investigation. Inside I found a marvelous Victorian floor laid out in red, green, white and yellow ceramic tiles (page 10). The design sprawled across the floor like a giant quilt. It almost made the announcement, "Look, I'm a quilt pattern!"

The Lincoln County Courthouse in Merrill, Wisconsin, has a sign in front of it indicating it was listed on the National Register of

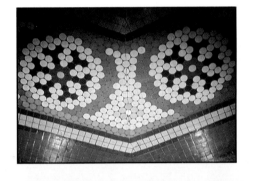

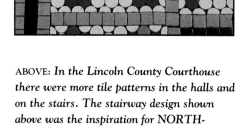

Historic Places. This was a definite clue that the interior of the building could have some interesting ornamentation. The ceramic tile floors inside had a variety of unique designs. There were two medallions or sunbursts, one much larger than the other, several border designs, plus some block patterns (pages 12-14). Thus, there was enough of an assortment of designs in the floors of just this one building to provide inspiration for several quilts.

Many old cafes, taverns, and restaurants have been remodeled, and often the owners have saved and refinished the original carved woodwork. Sometimes they have salvaged carved wood panels, back bars, and doors from other buildings that were destined to be torn down, and used them when they remodeled. Frequently these wood carvings used floral and leaf motifs as the theme of the design, and many of these can easily be simplified and adapted. There is a wealth of potential quilt patterns to be found in our old architecture, both inside and out. We must open our eyes and minds and allow our imaginations to go to work.

There are no firm rules which will tell you how to use this architectural gingerbread. Many times it is the location on the building that can provide the best clues. There might be single

ABOVE: *In the Lincoln County Courthouse there were more tile patterns in the halls and on the stairs. The stairway design shown above was the inspiration for NORTH-WOODS ROSE GARDEN, the wall quilt shown above left.*

OPPOSITE PAGE: *On a University of Minnesota building's concrete balustrade, shown at the top of the page, I found wonderful designs for a quilt pattern. However, this discovery took some detective work. Much of the decorative work on the building, as shown in the center photo, was hidden behind trees. The outline of this design was used as the pattern for a quilt border, as shown in the bottom photograph.*

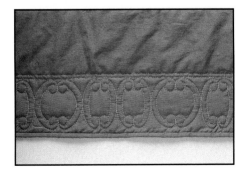

design units that can be used for blocks or medallion centers, or repeated designs that can be adapted into borders.

A variety of repeat patterns are often located along the roof edges, eaves, around doors or windows, and on tile floors. These can frequently be simplified, adapted, and used as the patterns for quilt borders or the setting strips between blocks. The designs around the doors, windows, and the edges of floors have usually been carefully laid out so they will turn a 45 degree angle without distorting or destroying any portion of the design. A photograph of the corners will depict how to adapt and draw the pattern for your quilt border.

Some wood or concrete balustrades on stairways, balconies, or along the tops of roofs have interesting repetitive designs, and because of this repetition, they should be examined for potential border adaptations. One example is a cast concrete balustrade on a building on the University of Minnesota campus. A few changes were made to it, and it became a distinctive quilted border pattern. Refer to photos on this page.

A single decorative unit of design frequently enhances the stone

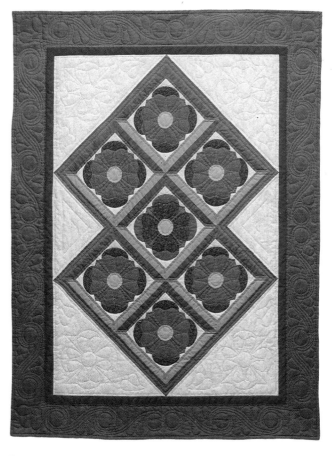

or tile fronts of fireplaces or appears on a heavy wood newel post on a staircase in homes or hotel lobbies. Some of these individual ornamental units are also set at intervals into the exterior surfaces of public buildings. Since these units are not connected to each other or to any other embellishment, they seem to be very appropriate patterns for quilt blocks or center medallions. Often their designs are simple and uncluttered so that they can be used for the quilt pattern almost the way they appear on the architecture with very little adaptation necessary. As an example, one of these units was used in A PATCH OF DOGWOOD BLOSSOMS crib quilt, as shown above. The seven flower blocks were inspired by the square terra cotta blocks located on the outside of the library building. Very few adaptations to the original architectural design were necessary. Other decorative units might have a more complex design, but with minimal simplification they can usually be adapted into one-of-a-kind block patterns. They are designs that will not be found in any pattern books.

Occasionally the ornamentation on an old building will be quite versatile and contain design that can be used for both block and border patterns. For example, the repeated design on the store

ABOVE: *From across the street, the Minneapolis library seemed to be an unlikely source for a quilt pattern. However close inspectation revealed terra cotta friezes and blocks like the one shown above. Both the applique pattern and border quilting design for A PATCH OF DOGWOOD BLOSSOMS evolved from this source.*

OPPOSITE PAGE: *This late 1880's Minneapolis store stands vacant. The terra cotta friezes that edge the windows and entrance contain several different design motifs which combined beautifully in my FLOWER GARDEN BORDER crib quilt.*

front shown on page 17 contains flowers and shapes that resemble a leaf or shell. The flowers can be separated from the rest of the border motif, and they can be modified into the pattern for an appliqued block or center medallion. They can also be used as an applique border or as the quilting pattern for a quilt's border. The decoration on this particular building has many possibilities. The design components could be used alone, in combinations, or as they appear on the building. Architectural details like these offer a real opportunity to let your imagination and creativity go to work.

The physical characteristics of stone and fabric are very different and yet the designs created for architecture can be changed to work with textiles. The designs that are cast in terra cotta or plaster, carved into stone, set in floor tiles, or cast in metal can be adapted and simplified for both applique and stitched quilt patterns.

Applique provides the quilter with the easiest technique for adapting architectural decorations. Its flexibility allows you to handle the numerous curves, twists, and irregular shapes found in these designs. The combination of natural and geometric forms can be interpreted in fabric to closely resemble the designs on the buildings. Small fabric pieces can be stitched on top of each other to

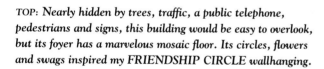

TOP: *Nearly hidden by trees, traffic, a public telephone, pedestrians and signs, this building would be easy to overlook, but its foyer has a marvelous mosaic floor. Its circles, flowers and swags inspired my FRIENDSHIP CIRCLE wallhanging.*

BOTTOM: *There is very little ornamentation on the exterior of this Duluth, Minnesota, mansion, but inside, the rectangular and square tiles in the fireplaces offered patterns for floral applique blocks like the one shown.*

form flower petals and leaves, and they can also be tucked under one another with relative ease, as shown on the opposite page. The round tiles in some of the floor designs seemed especially adaptable for English paper piecing. This technique will be used for the applique and it is explained in Chapter Six.

Architectural ornamentation can also be adapted for patterns to be used to quilt the layers of the quilt together. Many of the repetitive border designs found inside and outside of a building can be modified into the stitching patterns used for a quilt border. The shell or leaf shape is a common embellishment found on many buildings constructed during the Victorian era, and it can become a border pattern that is very different from any of the commercially made quilting stencils found in quilt shops, as shown below. This shell could also be quilted in the unpieced blocks found in the traditional quilt patterns such as the Double Irish Chain or Double Wedding Ring. Take a new look at old buildings and let their embellishments inspire you. They may provide you with exactly the pattern you need for your next quilt.

BOTTOM: Numerous bas relief sculptures, friezes and cartouches on this building are visible from the other side of the street. A single shell was the inspiration for a quilting stencil that was adapted for both block and border designs.

2
CHAPTER

ARCHITECTURAL PHOTOGRAPHY & RESOURCES

After you have become more aware of the potential quilt patterns that can be found in architectural embellishments, you will undoubtedly want to adapt some of them into quilts. But will you remember the details of that tile floor or that piece of molding you want to use? I doubt it. We all have a tendency to assume that our memories will retain all of these details, but in reality this just is not the case. So you will want some way to jog your memory when you are ready to start that quilt or wallhanging.

The next time you go into an area of your city or town where interesting buildings are located, carry a camera with you. You can photograph some of these old structures for future reference. You may even decide to plan a day of exploration within your city just to photograph decorative architecture. Usually no permission is needed to take pictures of exteriors of any public buildings, and in most cases, the interior foyers, lobbies, or hallways can also be photographed without permission. However, if you want to take a picture of some ornamentation that appears on either private property or inside a church, always obtain permission of the owner or clergy.

If you use a 35mm camera, either 200 Ektachrome™ slide or Kodacolor™ print film will give very satisfactory results: good color resolution outdoors, and even indoors, if a flash is used. Good quality black and white photos can be achieved by using Kodak TRI-X™. Many of the detail photos of the embellishments around doors or windows shown in this book were taken with a Nikon One Touch™ 35mm camera using 200 Ektachrome™ slide film and TRI-X™ black and white film. The architectural designs that appear along roof lines or up higher on the surface of the buildings were photographed with a Canon A-1™. The lens that was used was a 75 to 205 mm, 3.5f to 4.5f. Sometimes a 2x matched multiplier was added to get closer detail.

You will want clear photos to use for reference in adapting the design, but photo competition quality is not necessary. It is a good idea to take two pictures of each embellishment, just in case you move the camera accidentally. Try to take one direct or "head-on" shot. Sometimes structural objects or the location of the decorative piece can make it difficult or even impossible to do this, but try to take as nearly a direct shot as possible. You might try a slightly different angle for the second shot. When you take your pictures, notice if the design forms any right angles where it goes around a door or a window or where it forms the corner on the floor. Be sure to photograph that section. If you want to adapt this design for a quilt border, it will be especially helpful to have a photograph of that section. It is also helpful to have a 5" x 7" enlargement made from your print or slide. It is much easier to work from a larger photograph.

In small towns or rural settings, old buildings may be so scarce, that it is difficult to find some to photograph. Fortunately, there are other sources that can be used if you are interested in adapting architectural designs. Check your public library to see what books about architecture are available. Look especially for books about cathedrals, churches, Victorian houses, and Art Deco buildings. There may be quite a few good books on the subject. You can check them out to start planning that quilt right away. If you just want some pictures for future reference, the library probably has a photocopier available for public use. Although the photocopy will not be of the same quality as the photograph in the book or magazine, it will still provide an adequate reference. While you are at the library, look through issues of *National Geographic* and travel magazines. Very often they include photographs of buildings and cathedrals that may provide inspiration.

Newsstands and magazine counters usually carry several publications about architecture, such as *Architectural Digest*. These can be helpful as references you will not have to return to the library in two weeks. Frequently newsstands also have a display rack of post cards. You can look at these for any pictures of architectural subjects. Post cards can be an especially good purchase when you are traveling. The professional photographer is able to take close-up photos that you may not be able to obtain with your camera equipment.

Pictures, photographs, and magazines will help you build an excellent reference file on architectural ornamentations. It is very convenient to have this resource within reach when you want to make a quilt that will be very original and special. A section of black and white photographs and a list of suggested reading are included at the end of this book.

SECTION II

ADAPTING DECORATIVE DESIGNS

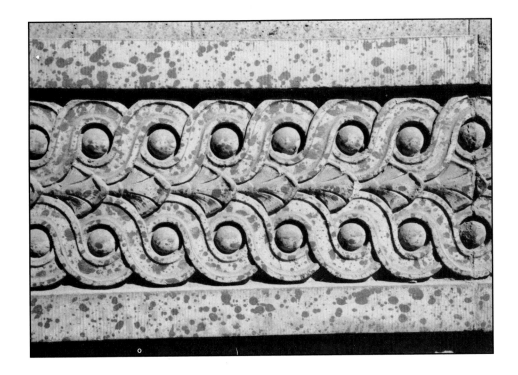

3
CHAPTER

DRAWING THE PATTERN

You may have found some embellishment that especially appeals to you, and now you would like to adapt it into a quilt pattern. The next step is making the drawing for your pattern from the photograph or picture.

Analyze the decoration very carefully. Would it work best as a block or border pattern? Will it be done in applique or as the quilted pattern? Architectural designs are often too elaborate to use exactly as they appear on a building. Some of the details may have to be eliminated or changed to make it easier to applique. If there are twelve petals on a flower, can you create the illusion with only five or six? Remember, teeny, tiny pieces of fabric are difficult to hold in place while you stitch, and they may also fray as you work.

Perhaps the general outline of the flower will help you determine the number and shape of the petals you need to make the flower resemble the original one on the building. Are the leaf edges notched with numerous indentations? Try reducing the number of notches or smoothing out the edges. Does the center of the blossom have too many stamens? Perhaps they could be replaced with a plain circle. Possibly, your choice of the fabric could give the feeling of the stamens. The idea is to capture the essence of the piece of ornamentation rather than try to make an exact fabric duplicate. If some of the elements of the design are too tiny to use, consider enlarging them or eliminating them altogether. Remember, once again, you are going to applique these pieces, and this should be fun! Do not make the pieces so small that you will become frustrated. Use your imagination, and be creative. You want to end up with a drawing that you can use to make your actual templates, not a drawing for an art exhibition.

The drawing must be made to the exact size that you want to use in your quilt because you will use it to make your templates. If you are able to do a free-hand drawing, you are ready to start. If you think that is too difficult, there are several methods that can help you with the drawing process. These methods can be used to help you draw the patterns for either applique blocks and borders or for quilted blocks and borders.

DRAWING PATTERNS FOR BLOCKS

If you have an accurate slide of the architectural detail, you can enlarge it by using a slide projector to project the image onto a sheet of paper. Draw the outline dimensions of your quilt block or center medallion on a sheet of drawing paper or newsprint. Attach the paper to a wall with masking tape. Place the slide projector at the proper distance from the wall and project the architectural image to fit within your block size. Then use a pencil and draw around the image. The paper can be moved or rotated as necessary to develop your drawing. *Do not* use a permanent marker for this step. It could bleed through the paper and damage the wall. If you have a direct or head-on view of the design, the image will be a fairly accurate enlargement. Even if your slide is not that accurate in its perspective, it may still be good enough to allow you to "even things up" later freehand. It is important to be as accurate as possible, but remember that you are not doing microsurgery. You are permitted to change, adjust, delete, or move a line or shape however you wish if doing so simplifies the design or makes it more graceful. The amount of time that the slide is exposed to the bright light of the projector bulb should not be long enough to damage it. If you are concerned about damage to the slide, turn the projector off for a few minutes and allow it to cool.

If you have photos or pictures instead of slides, the same method can be used with an opaque projector. This equipment can sometimes be found at the library or at a school. Check with the librarian or school principal to see if you can use it for a half hour or so. The opaque projector may curl up your original photo or picture because of the heat it generates, but generally the photo or picture will flatten out nicely, especially if it is placed under a couple of books.

The use of tracing paper can be very helpful for making changes on your drawings while you work. Instead of erasing or re-drawing your pattern, cover it with a sheet of tracing paper. The original drawing will be visible underneath so you will be able to make the modifications and adjustments without doing damage to the origi-

nal. When you are satisfied with your changes, either staple or tape the tracing paper to your original drawing or just use this new one.

There is still another method that can be used to enlarge the photo or picture when you make your drawing: the grid method. Most quilters are familiar with this technique. To do this, the original photo or picture must be divided into a grid composed of small squares; usually the number of large squares in the block must be exactly the same as the number of small squares. For example, if the original photo is divided into twelve ½" squares vertically and twelve ½" squares horizontally, your block outline will also have to be divided into twelve larger squares vertically and twelve larger squares horizontally. Refer to photo above. The size of these larger squares will be determined by the size of your finished block.

Drawing the grid lines directly onto the photo or onto the picture would do permanent damage. To prevent this, I cover my photos with an 8½" x 11" transparent plastic grid. I made some grids with a fine line marker on sheets of white paper. One grid had ¼" squares and the other had ½" squares. These sheets were photocopied onto overhead projector transparency plastic as shown above right. The lines on the plastic copies are permanent. They will not smear or rub off as marker lines tend to do on plastic. These grids are reusable and I can use them whenever I want to enlarge any drawing or picture. Patterns for these two grids are included at the end of Section Four so you can make photocopies of them.

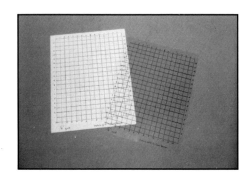

The image is transferred square by square from the smaller grid to the larger one. A grid was drawn on white paper and then photocopied onto acetate sheets (the ones used to make transparencies for use with an overhead projector).

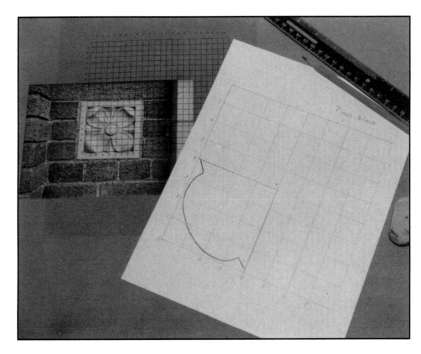

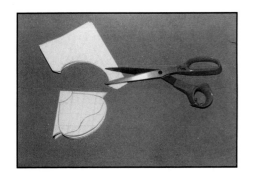

Only one quarter of a symmetrical flower is drawn into the large grid. The grid with the drawing was folded into quarters and cut out. The details were drawn for just one petal and one leaf, and the center circle was completed.

Place a zero in the bottom left corner on both the small and large grids. Number the lines consecutively, vertically and horizontally, on both of these grids. Now transfer the picture from the photo to your block by duplicating the images that appear within each small square to the corresponding larger squares. This might seem tedious, but it does have the advantage of letting you simplify and adjust the design as you make the transfer. You may realize as you draw that some of the pieces will be too little to applique unless you change them.

DRAWING SYMMETRICAL PATTERNS

Many of the single floral designs seem to have four symmetrical petals, and they can almost be duplicated just as they appear on the building. This makes the grid technique easier because it is not necessary to draw each of the four identical petals or leaves. Refer to the terra cotta square that appears on the library building on page 16, and to the photographs in the last section of the book. Prepare the two grids as described, but only transfer and draw one quarter of the embellishment into the larger grid square, as shown above right. Fold this drawing into quarters and cut along the pencil line. When you unfold it, you will have a symmetrical cutout or silhouette of the flower. This cutout silhouette will be used to make the applique templates. Draw all details of the pattern into only one of the petals. Refer to photographs on this page. The cutout silhouette can also be used to make a template for marking the applique outline onto your block or background fabric.

This method can be used to adapt a shape such as a leaf or one of the flowers in the terra cotta trim on the Minneapolis store front border shown on page 17. Perhaps you found a floral shape or a leaf that you would like to use, but you want to use it in a different way than it was shown in the architectural design. Refer to the FLOWER GARDEN BORDER quilt also shown on page 17. The buds, flowers, and leaves were rearranged and spaced differently from their original placement on the building trim. Individual drawings were made for each of them.

Decide what size flower or leaf you want to use in your block or border, and use the two grids. Transfer only one half of the flower or leaf from the smaller grid to the larger grid. Fold the grid in half, as if you were going to cut out a paper valentine. Cut out the drawing, and when it is unfolded, you will have a complete leaf or flower. Duplicating the details into the other half of the silhouette is easy, too. Re-fold it on the crease, and hold it against a window. The original pencil lines will show through both layers of paper so you can trace them on the other half. When the drawing is unfolded, both halves should be identical.

OPPOSITE: *The edges of the drawing were folded over each other to make a continuous pattern. The grid was planned for a 6″ border, with each ¼″ equaling ¾″.*

DRAWING THE PATTERNS FOR BORDERS

A slide projector or opaque projector can also be used to make your border drawing. Draw two horizontal lines the width of your border on paper. Remember, to allow a ¼″ for any seams, if applicable, and for the bound edge. This means a 6″ border may only have 5 or 5½ inches of pattern space. The length of these two horizontal lines should be long enough to allow several repeats of the pattern. Tape this paper to a wall and project the image to fit between the two horizontal lines. Draw around the designs with a pencil until you reach the end of the lines. Be sure you have drawn all of the sections of the design before you take down the paper, and remember to do all of the drawing with a pencil.

When the drawing has been completed, the left and the right ends of the border will have to be adjusted so that the ends of the pattern will line up with each other. The pattern has to continue smoothly and accurately from end to end as you transfer it onto the quilt border. Draw a vertical line on the left edge where you started the drawing, and draw another vertical line on the right edge where you finished it. Cut along these two vertical lines to even up the edges and get rid of the excess paper. Place the drawing upside down

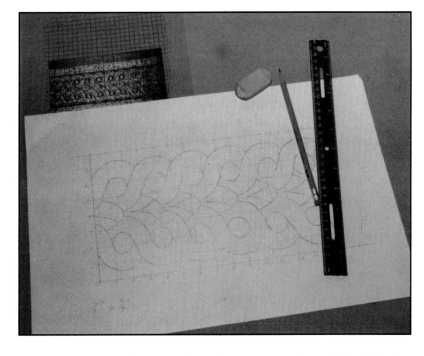

and fold the left edge over the right. Refer to photo left. Slide the right edge under the left one until the patterns line up with each other. Draw a vertical line where this occurs. When you unfold the paper, cut on this line to get rid of the portion that did not match up. This remaining section of your drawing will be used to make the applique or quilting template. If you wish to make the drawing longer, use tracing paper to do additional repeats of your pattern.

The design can also be enlarged using the grid method explained in an earlier paragraph. Make the grid to fit the pattern width of the quilt's border, as shown above. The length is not as important, just as long as you draw several repeats of the architectural design unit. After several units have been transferred to your larger grid, draw the vertical lines at either end of the drawing. Cut along these vertical lines to get the excess paper out of your way. Place the drawing upside down and fold the left edge over the right edge. Slide the right one under the left edge until the drawings line up with each other. Draw a vertical line along the edge where this occurs. Unfold the drawing and cut on this line. Once again, if you want to make your drawing longer, use a sheet of tracing paper to copy the image.

Your drawing is your most important step in adapting the design from a building into a pattern for a quilt. It should be accurate and it should not be cut apart. It will receive much use in the next chapters as you make your templates and quilting stencils, so keep it handy, but safe.

4
CHAPTER

MAKING APPLIQUE TEMPLATES

W̶hen the final drawing has been completed, you are ready to make the applique templates. The drawing should be the exact size to fit the finished block, center medallion, or border, and it should be drawn exactly as you want the applique pattern to look. The templates will be made from that drawing.

There are a few supplies you will need to make the templates: plastic template material, a pencil, an eraser, a small sharp pair of scissors for cutting the plastic, a fine tip permanent marker, masking tape, and your drawing.

Draw over your final drawing with a permanent marker to darken the lines. These lines will be the outlines of the template pattern pieces. After the marker has dried, erase any unwanted pencil lines that will cause confusion when the pattern pieces are being traced onto the template material. The inked lines should be very clear and precise, because the template pieces will be traced off them.

Tape the drawing onto a smooth flat surface to keep it from slipping. Cover it with a sheet of template plastic, and tape that down securely also. If your drawing or template plastic shifts while you are tracing, your patterns will be inaccurate. You should be able to see the darkened lines of your drawing through the template plastic. Use a pencil and trace the lines of the drawing onto the plastic. When each part of the drawing has been transferred onto the plastic, the tape can be removed. Label or number the pieces on both your original drawing and the template plastic drawing so that the numbers match. Cut the template plastic apart very carefully, following your pencil lines. It is very important that you *do not* cut apart your original drawing. It is your only guide to reassembling these pieces when you applique them onto the background fabric. This drawing will also be used to make a silhouette template which will be used to transfer the pattern outline onto your block, medallion, or border fabric.

Some quilters like to use the cardboard template – spray starch – iron applique technique, developed by Helen Kelley, to form the fabric pieces of the applique. If this technique is going to be used, the drawing will have to be transferred onto cardboard instead of the plastic template material. The plastic material would melt from the heat of the iron when the fabric pieces are pressed over the edges of the template. You will need some additional supplies for this method: a sheet of railroad or tag board, a ball point pen or stylus, small scissors for cutting the cardboard, masking tape and a sheet of yellow dressmaker's tracing paper. Dressmaker's tracing paper is found in the notion department of most fabric stores, and there is an assortment of colors in each package. Although the package is labeled dressmaker's tracing paper, it actually resembles a colored carbon paper and not a translucent tracing paper. One side of the sheet has a waxy surface, and the other side feels like plain paper. Because of this, I will refer to it in this book as dressmaker's carbon paper. Be sure that the paper you use has a waxy side. The yellow sheet will be used for making cardboard templates because it will not discolor your fabric if a little yellow residue remains on the edges of your applique templates after you cut them out of cardboard.

Tape the cardboard down securely to a smooth flat surface. Cover the cardboard with your drawing, and secure it along three sides with masking tape. Slip the dressmaker's carbon paper between the cardboard and your drawing with the waxy surface resting on the cardboard. *Do not* tape this sheet down. It may be necessary to move the dressmaker's carbon paper as you work because it might not be large enough to cover the entire piece of cardboard. This will not cause any problems if both the cardboard and your drawing are taped securely. Using a ball point pen or stylus, trace over the lines on your original drawing. This will transfer them onto the cardboard. When this step has been completed, the cardboard can be carefully cut apart on the yellow lines. These are the applique template pieces and they should be numbered or labeled to match the drawing.

If you are drawing a symmetrical design or one that uses the same leaf or shape several times within the pattern, it is not necessary to make duplicate templates of each of these parts. For example, the four petals of the flower in A PATCH OF DOGWOOD BLOSSOMS are identical, as shown on page 16. Simply make one template for a petal, one for the leaf, and another for the flower center, as shown right. These templates can be used again many times. If they do become bent from the iron, you still have your original drawing to use to make replacements.

Many quilters are familiar with the freezer paper technique used for applique. This technique has become a very popular method of shaping or forming the fabric applique pieces because of its accuracy. You will need a roll of freezer paper which is available at most supermarkets. Cut a piece that is the same size as your drawing. Tape it to a smooth, flat surface, with the waxy side of the freezer paper facing downward. Put your drawing over it and tape it down on three sides. Place a yellow sheet of dressmaker's carbon paper between the drawing and the freezer paper. Trace over the lines of your drawing. When this process is complete, cut the freezer paper image apart on the yellow lines. These paper pieces are the templates. They will be pinned, waxy side up, on the wrong side of your fabric. The fabric pieces will be cut out with a ¼" seam allowance. The seam allowance will be ironed over the edge of the freezer paper. The fabric will adhere to the waxy finish and the applique piece will be shaped just as you need it. The freezer paper templates can be used several times before you need to replace them.

When all of the templates for the applique have been made, your original drawing will be used to transfer the pattern onto your background fabric. This is the reason why you never cut up that drawing. If your background fabric is a light-colored solid, you may be able to see your drawing through it. If so, tape the drawing onto a smooth, flat surface. Align the fabric over it with the right side facing up, and tape it down with masking tape. Use a pencil or your favorite marking tool, and trace only the outline of the design onto the background fabric. Do this very lightly. This is the guide to positioning the fabric applique pieces for stitching.

If you are unable to see through your fabric clearly, you can use a light box or a window to transfer the design. Tape both the drawing and fabric down securely to either the surface of the light box or to a window pane. Do the tracing with either a silver or white pencil or your favorite marking tool.

If your background fabric is dark, the drawing can be transferred by using a sheet of white dressmaker's carbon paper. The white dressmaker's carbon paper is the *only* color that should be used for this purpose because it will not leave any color residue. When all of

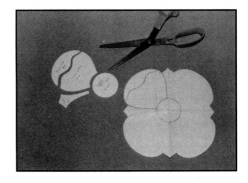

ABOVE: *Applique templates are made by tracing the drawing onto template plastic.*

ABOVE: *A silhouette template is made from the drawing and is used to transfer the outline on the block.*

the applique has been completed and the piece is pressed, any white lines not completely covered by the applique pieces will disappear. This is *not* true of the other colored sheets of carbon paper. The wax will melt, but the colored dyes will remain behind, and I do not know how they can be removed! The best suggestion I can give is to remove all of those colored sheets from the package and put them away where you will not be tempted to use them. Press your background fabric before you transfer your drawing with the white dressmaker's carbon because you cannot iron it again until the applique work has been finished. Tape the fabric to a smooth flat surface with the right side up, and tape your drawing over it securely. Slip the white carbon paper between the fabric and the drawing with the waxy side resting on the fabric. Use a ballpoint pen or stylus and trace over your drawing. You can slide the carbon paper as necessary to transfer the outline of your design. When the outline is transferred, everything can be untaped. Remember, you will not be able to iron it after you transfer the pattern with white carbon paper or you will melt away the outlines.

You can also make a silhouette template of your drawing which you can use to transfer the pattern onto the fabric. Place a piece of plastic template material over your drawing. The plastic should be large enough to cover the entire pattern. Trace *only* the outline of the pattern onto the plastic. Cut it out carefully, inside your lines. Place this silhouette on the right side of your fabric, and trace around it using your favorite marking tool, as shown left.

MAKING QUILTING STENCILS

There are some embellishments or designs that seem to be more easily adapted for the quilting patterns than for applique patterns. Some of these will work best as the stitching patterns for quilt borders, whereas others will make interesting patterns to stitch into other areas of the quilt. The repeat patterns found along the edges of eaves, around entrances, or girdling exterior surfaces can usually be simplified and adapted into unique patterns that can be quilted on either the border or the setting strips of a quilt. A design that is carved into a spandrel or a panel above a door might be a perfect one to stitch elsewhere on the quilt, such as in the plain blocks or corner triangles. The location of the ornament on the building itself can be the best clue for its use in quilting.

You will need to make a stencil to mark the quilting lines onto your quilt top. The stencil will be made from the drawing you have just completed. This drawing should have been made the exact size to fit your border or block. The methods for enlarging the architectural decoration were described in Chapter Three.

Analyze the decorative piece thoroughly. Usually it has to be simplified quite a bit when it is going to be used for the quilt stitching. When an embellishment is adapted for applique, it can be more complex. Several colors are used in the applique and they define the pattern. However, if there is too much detail in your quilting pattern, it will become a jumble of stitches. It will become difficult to distinguish the pattern from the rest of the quilting. If there are too many veins within the leaves, it will be hard to pick out the actual leaf shape. This does not mean you cannot do a lot of quilting. Stipple quilting in some areas will make the background recess and the pattern become raised and accented. It simply means you will have

RIGHT: *Silhouette stencils include only the outline of patterns.*

to analyze the embellishment thoroughly to decide what part can be used and what part must be eliminated. When you have done that and you have made a satisfactory drawing, you are ready to make the stencils. Use a fine tip permanent marker and darken the pencil lines on your drawing so that they can be clearly seen through a sheet of template plastic.

There are several kinds of quilting stencils that can be made. There is a silhouette or outline stencil, and the negative silhouette or negative outline stencil. There is another style resembling the commercially made ones found in quilt shops. It has the design cut or drilled into a large rectangle or square of plastic template material. Lastly, stencils can be made by combining the silhouette stencil with a cut or drilled stencil. Your finished drawing should help you determine which type of stencil will be best suited for your pattern.

A silhouette stencil is the easiest and probably the fastest type to make. An example is shown above. Tape your final drawing onto a smooth, flat surface, and tape a sheet of template plastic over it. The darkened lines of your drawing should be visible through the plastic. Using a pencil, trace the outline of your drawing onto the template plastic. When the entire outline has been transferred, cut the plastic out carefully along the pencil lines with small scissors. Old manicure or embroidery scissors work well for this. If the design contains some circles or ovals that need to have their centers removed, cut a slit into those center sections. Cut out the unwanted centers. Then tape the slit closed with a bit of transparent tape. This method is much safer, easier, and more accurate than trying to poke a starting hole into the plastic with either the tip of the scissors or the point of a knife.

The silhouette stencil is easy to use, too, because you can see all around its edges. Place it on the area of the quilt you want to mark. It can be held into position with either a couple of long quilter's pins straddling the stencil or with two or three tiny pieces of masking tape placed along its edge. Trace around the stencil very lightly, using a pencil or your favorite marking tool.

The negative silhouette stencil is very similar to the other silhouette style. It works well with designs that have thin elongations such as vines or stems, or sections of a design that are not attached to the main unit of the design. A piece of plastic template material is cut into a square or a rectangle about 1" larger than your pattern. This will leave a margin of template plastic around the edges to provide some strength to the stencil, as shown right. Trace the outline of your drawing on it. Cut the design out of the rectangle or square carefully. This opening or cutout in the plastic material is the stencil used to mark the pattern on your quilt.

A negative silhouette stencil is cut within a large piece of template material.

The third type of quilting stencil is a bit more difficult to cut, but it can be well worth the trouble for more complex designs, particularly if they have many curves. Again, transfer the design onto the plastic material by taping both your final drawing and the plastic to a smooth, flat surface. Trace the pattern through the plastic with a pencil. After the entire drawing has been transferred onto the plastic, cut thin channels into it following your pencil lines. Use either a very sharp craft knife or an electric stencil cutting tool, if you own one. It is a good idea to protect the surface underneath with heavy cardboard or a rotary cutter mat. If you use a knife, it can be difficult to cut completely through the plastic without using some pressure, so caution should be taken to prevent cutting yourself.

If you own an electric hand drill or a Dremel Moto Tool™, this kind of stencil can be made very easily, without the danger of a sharp knife blade causing injury. Instead of cutting channels, a series of holes are drilled at intervals into the plastic. After your design has been traced onto the template plastic, tape it onto an old piece of wood or several thicknesses of *very* heavy cardboard. This will protect your work surface from being damaged by the tip of the drill bit. Using a very fine drill bit in either the electric drill or the Moto Tool™, drill tiny holes into the plastic through your pencil lines. These holes should be spaced about ¼" apart. The finished stencil will resemble a child's dot-to-dot picture, in the outline of your design, as shown below left.

To use this type of stencil, position the template exactly over the area of your quilt to be marked. Use two or three little pieces of masking tape to hold it into place. Mark each dot onto the quilt top through the holes in the template with a pencil that has a fine lead, or use your favorite marking tool. You can either connect these dots with a pencil line or with quilt stitches as you go.

The silhouette stencil can also have holes drilled into it or channels cut into it, which makes a fourth style of marking device. Refer to the photograph below. Transfer the drawing onto a piece of template plastic using the method previously described. Carefully cut out the silhouette or outline shape. Then, using a drill, Moto Tool™, knife, or electric stencil cutting tool, make a series of holes or channels through your pencil lines within the inside of the silhouette shape.

As you draw and adapt your design, you will be able to decide which type of stencil will work the best for the area of your quilt you need to mark. These will be unique patterns custom designed to fit your quilt.

A drilled or channel cut stencil provides more pattern detail. A stencil can also be a combination of types – a silhouette with holes or channels.

SECTION III

QUILT PATTERNS

TULIP STAR

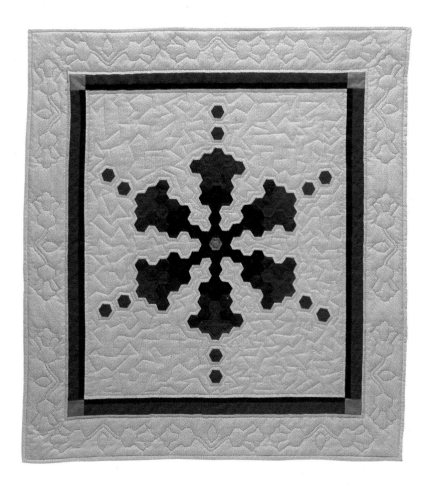

LEFT: *TULIP STAR, 33" x 36", designed and appliqued by the author, 1990. Hand quilted by Lori Olsson, Maplewood, MN. Refer to page 45 for layout.*
Photo: Benkert Photography.

ABOVE: *Close-up of the inspiration, a red and green tile pattern on a white background.*

When I discovered the old tile floor shown above right, I immediately thought of how much it resembled a quilt. The pattern created by the red and green tiles would not be difficult to duplicate in fabric, and the colors reminded me of the Christmas season. I decided to use just one of the pattern units as the design for a small quilt (33" x 36") that could be used as either a holiday wallhanging or table center piece. I decided that the English paper piecing technique would be an easy way to make this pattern.

It would have been possible to make the entire quilt top out of English paper pieced hexagons, but I wanted to applique the design unit onto a seamless background. It would also be easier to attach the narrow red and green borders, and be much easier to quilt a random pattern if there were no seams to stitch across in the background fabric.

SUPPLIES:
2⅛ yd. background fabric
½ yd. red solid
¼ yd. medium green solid
¼ yd. dark green print
¼ yd. dark green solid for the border
⅛ yd. gold solid
1 spool each, red and green sewing thread
White thread, for basting
1 spool each, gray and black quilting thread
Quilt batting, about 34" x 37"
Basic sewing supplies
Several sheets of 8½" x 11" lightweight paper
Plastic template material

ENGLISH PAPER PIECING:
The English paper piecing technique shapes the fabric hexagon by folding the piece of cloth over the edges of a paper hexagon. One paper hexagon is required for each hexagon in your pattern.

1. Trace the hexagon pattern provided at left onto template plastic. You need to make only one plastic template.

2. Place the template on one of the sheets of paper, and carefully draw around it. You can draw 20 hexagons on one sheet of paper, and make five additional copies of it on a photocopier. This will give you enough hexagons for this pattern. If you decide to use a photocopier, allow at least a 1" margin all around the edge of the paper. It is a good idea to check your first photocopy against your original for accuracy. If you decide to trace each of the hexagons by hand, you must make 115 of them.

3. Cut the sheets of hexagons apart carefully.

Hexagon pattern for English paper piecing.

4. Pin them to the WRONG side of your applique fabrics, as shown in A. Allow about ¼" around each of them for seams.

5. Cut out the fabrics with the papers pinned to them, allowing that ¼" seam to extend beyond the edges of the papers, as in B.

6. Carefully fold the seam allowance over the edge of the paper hexagon. Baste the paper onto the fabric so that the knot will be exposed on the right side of the fabric. It will be so much easier to remove all of the basting threads later if you see the knots.

7. Continue basting around the remaining five edges, folding the fabric as you go. Refer to C.

8. Cover all of the hexagons this way. You will need 42 red, 36 medium green, 36 dark green print, and 1 gold.

9. When all of the hexagons are covered, lay them out in the shape of the quilt pattern. You will find this helpful when you start sewing them together.

10. Pick up two hexagons, and place one on top of the other with the right sides together. Using thread to match, whipstitch them together along one edge of each hexagon, as shown in D. Sew through only one or two threads on each of the two edges. This whipstitch will make a hinge between the two hexagons. Try not to sew into the paper inside, though it will not cause any problems if you accidently do.

11. After sewing a pair of hexagons together, fasten the thread. Open them out, flat. If your stitches are small, they should not show on the right side.

12. Assemble the additional pairs and whipstitch them together to make a flower unit as they are shown on page 43 and 45.

13. Repeat these steps to make the remaining five units. You should have one gold and 12 single red hexagons left over. Do not remove any papers yet.

14. Attach the six flower units to the center gold hexagon. The flower pattern and the 12 single hexagons are now ready to applique to the background fabric.

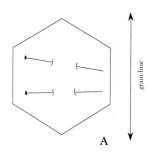

A

grain line

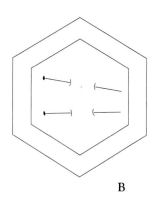

B

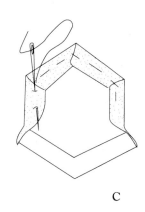

C

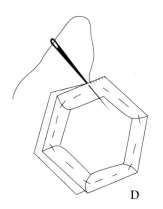

D

CONSTRUCTING THE TOP:

All measurements have been given without seam allowance. Add ¼".

1. Cut a 22" x 25" rectangle out of the background fabric. Also cut two 4" x 33" borders and two 4" x 36" borders in this same fabric. Cut the backing or lining at this time also. It should be a little larger than the completed top, or about 34" x 37". Remember those seam allowances!

2. Cut two strips, ½" x 22", and two strips, ½" x 25" out of the green border fabric. Be sure to add seams.

3. Cut two strips, 1" x 22", and two strips, 1" x 25" out of red fabric. Seams must be added.

4. Cut four 1½" gold squares, plus seams.

5. Center the flower applique on the background rectangle. Baste it into position so it will not shift while you applique. Applique into place, changing the thread colors when necessary as you stitch.

6. When the entire applique has been stitched into place, the single hexagons can be appliqued into place on the background. Place the first hexagon ¾" from the tip of one of the flower units, and applique into place. Place the second hexagon 2½" away from the flower tip and applique. Repeat with the remaining ten hexagons and five flower tips.

7. Sew the 22" red and green strips together and press. Sew a 1½" gold square to each end of this border.

8. Sew the remaining 25" red and green strips together and press.

9. Refer to the color photo of the quilt for placement and sew the 25" borders to the 25" edges of the rectangle and press.

10. Sew the remaining borders to the edges of the center rectangle.

11. Attach the four background fabric borders. Miter the corners. This completes the assembly of the quilt top, and the paper hexagons should still be inside the applique at this time.

OPOSITE PAGE: English Paper Piecing. Paper is pinned to wrong side of fabric. A ¼" seam is added to the fabric hexagons as they are cut out. The edges of the fabric are folded and basted to the paper. With right sides together, the two edges are whipstitched together.

BELOW: Hexagons stitched into tulip shapes.

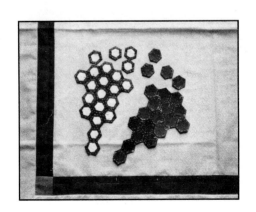

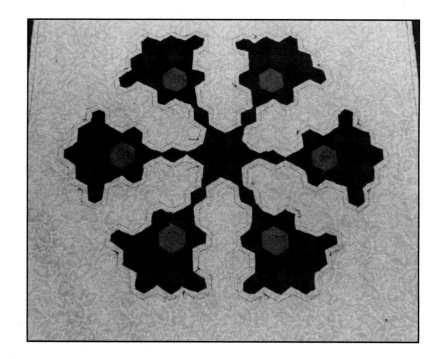

REMOVING THE PAPERS:

1. Remove *all* of the basting stitches from the applique.

2. Turn the quilt top over so that the wrong side is facing you.

3. With the tip of your scissors, carefully make a starting hole under the applique. Cut away the background fabric underneath the applique. Allow a ¼" seam from the edge of the applique stitches. This will expose the paper hexagons.

4. Remove these papers by lifting them away from the fabric. If they are stitched to the applique, a gentle pull will tear them free without tearing the stitches. When all of the papers have been removed, the top will look like the example shown above. Press the top.

QUILTING:

Two colors of quilting thread were used to quilt this piece. Gray was used to quilt the background around the flower applique. Black was used within the applique and in the outer border, as shown right. The background was outline quilted ¼" around the edges of the applique, and ¼" from the edge of the green border. The remaining background was filled in with random, wandering lines of quilting. No quilting stencil was used in the center rectangle. Refer to the diagram on page 45 for the quilting design used within the applique.

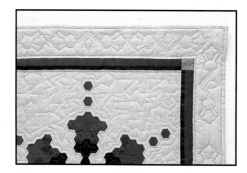

ABOVE: *This is a detail of the quilting in the tulips, background, and borders. Photo: Benkert Photography.*

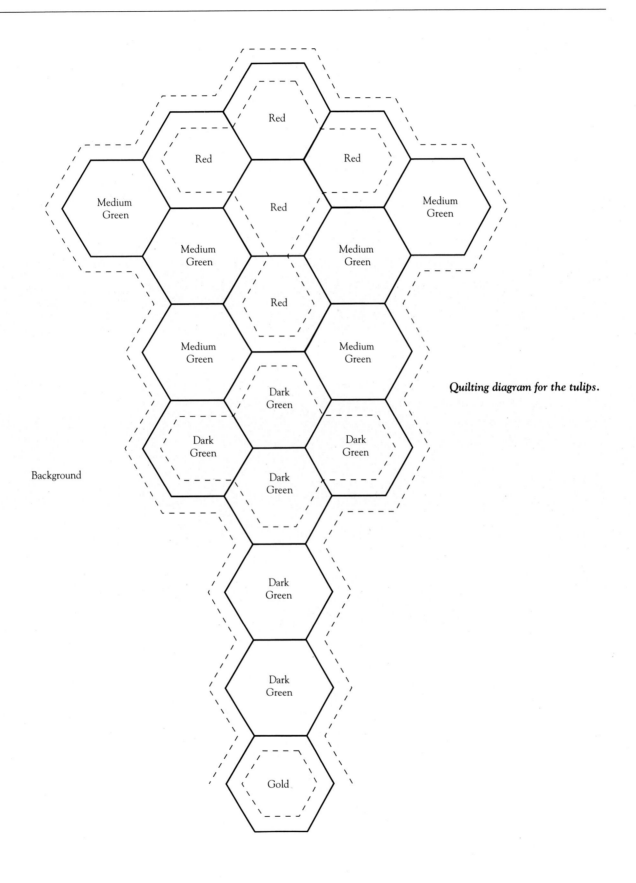

Quilting diagram for the tulips.

Background

The quilting design for the border was adapted from the flower pattern. A drawing was done to resemble the outline of one of the flowers. A negative silhouette stencil was made from the drawing, as shown right. The plastic template material was cut 4" wide, the width of the border, and the silhouette was centered in it. The stencil was then self-centering when it was placed on the border for marking.

After the outline was traced onto the border, a smaller stencil was placed inside the outline and traced to indicate the blossom outline.

ABOVE: *The negative silhouette stencil made from the drawing.*

MARKING THE BORDER PATTERN

1. Use the method described in Chapter Four to make the quilting stencils out of the template plastic. The patterns are provided on page 47.

2. Find the middle of the 33" border. Center the stencil over this mark, and trace the silhouette using your favorite marking tool.

3. Pick up the stencil and move it to the right. Allow about ½" between the ends of the outlines. Position it and trace. Repeat this step on the left side of this border.

4. Trace the blossom outlines by placing the smaller stencil over the ends of the flowers. Draw around the sides and bottom of this stencil.

5. Pick up the stencil and move it to the 36" border. Repeat step two, but this time allow about 2" between the outlines. Trace.

6. Repeat steps three and four. Complete the marking of these remaining borders in this manner.

7. Mark a quilting line on the background rectangle ¼" from the green border.

8. Mark a quilting line on the background border ¼" from the red border.

9. Prepare the three layers for quilting and then begin quilting.

10. When all of the quilting has been completed, bind the edges with fabric to match the background.

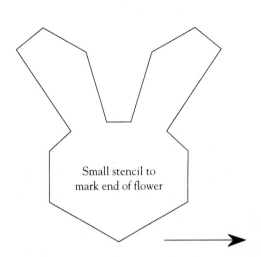

Small stencil to
mark end of flower

§ B § in stencil patterns
indicates an area where
a "bridge" is left between
the sides of the stencil to
strengthen it.

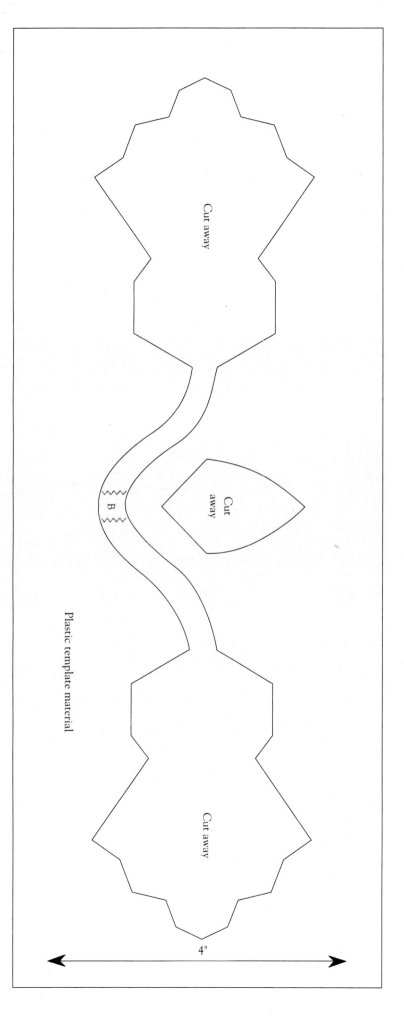

Cut away

Cut
away

B

Plastic template material

Cut away

4"

A Patch Of Dogwood Blossoms

RIGHT: *A terra cotta block and frieze embellishing a public library's exterior became the inspiration for a crib quilt.*

LEFT: A PATCH OF DOGWOOD BLOSSOMS, *38" x 50¾", designed and appliqued by the author, 1990; hand quilted by Jeanne Tanamachi, Lauderdale, MN. Photo: Benkert Photography.*

The inspiration for this crib quilt came from the embellishments found on a public library building. The appliqued blocks were adapted from small terra cotta squares located on the building's exterior walls. There were several border decorations around the windows and the door that could be used for quilting designs. It was necessary to decide how many of the library designs I would use on this small quilt.

As the terra cotta embellishments were located about nine feet above ground level, it was not possible to take a photograph without some distortion. I was not able to get up high enough to be directly in front of the flower or border to obtain a slide or photo that I could project. My drawing for the quilt pattern would have to be done freehand from my snapshot.

Very few changes were made to the original square terra cotta flower design. Each of my quilt blocks was 9" square and that included a one-inch border. The border was included in the block dimensions to replicate the narrow edge around the architectural square. One half of that border was dark gray and the other half light gray, to create the effect of shadows. The flower was symmetrical, which greatly simplified the freehand drawing process.

A seven-inch square was cut out of a piece of lightweight paper and then folded into eighths. One-half of one leaf and one-half of one petal were drawn onto the folded edges, as shown right. When the drawing was cut along the pencil lines and unfolded, the pattern was symmetrical. This technique was described in Chapter Three. I made a silhouette template from my cutout so that I could trace that outline onto the background fabric of each block. The folded drawing was also used to make templates for the applique.

ABOVE: *The pattern was drawn on folded paper to make it symmetrical.*

RIGHT: *Pattern for the applique templates and silhouette template. Pattern pieces are numbered in the order in which they are appliqued.*

SUPPLES

2⅝ yds. block background and backing fabric
1⅝ yds. gray solid for borders and binding
1⅜ yds. deep burgundy solid
¼ yd. light gray solid
¼ yd. dark rose print
⅜ yd. medium rose to pink print
⅛ yd. light pink solid
⅜ yd. green solid
Thread to match applique
Plastic template material
Gray quilting thread
Marking pencil
Crib-size batt, 45" x 60"
Basic sewing supplies

BLOCK CONSTRUCTION
All measurements have been given without seam allowance. Add ¼".

1. Cut seven 7" squares out of your background fabric, plus seams.

2. Cut 14 light gray strips 1" x 9", and 14 dark gray strips 1" x 9"; add seams.

3. Sew two light and two dark strips onto each 7" square. Miter the corners and press. You should now have seven 9" blocks.

APPLIQUE
1. Make applique templates from the pattern on page 51. You will need to make only one template for the leaf, one for the inner part

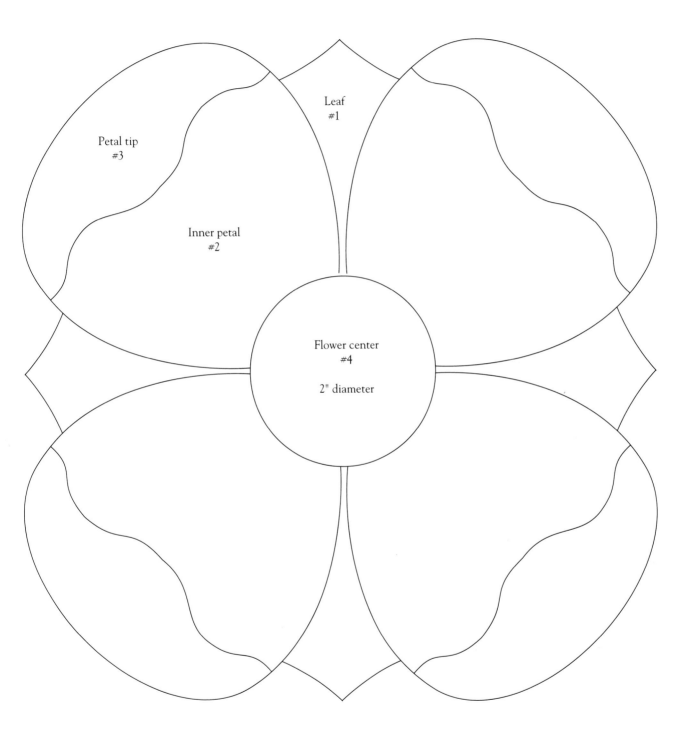

Leaf
#1

Petal tip
#3

Inner petal
#2

Flower center
#4

2" diameter

of the petal, one for the petal tip, and one for the flower center.

2. Cut the following applique pieces from your fabric:
    24 rose inner petals
    24 dark rose petal tips
    28 green leaves
    7 flower centers
    4 dark rose inner petals
    4 rose petal tips

3. Trace the outline of the leaf template on the right side of the green fabric leaf pieces so that this line can be used as a guide to position the sides of the petals.

4. Make a silhouette template of the applique pattern on template plastic.

5. Center this template on the blocks and trace around it.

6. Place the leaves on the outline traced on the block. Accurately align the top of the leaves with the outline. Applique into place.

7. Place the petal pieces on the block so their sides will line up with the lines drawn on the edge of the leaf pieces. Applique in the numerical sequence given on the pattern.

8. Repeat steps five through seven with the remaining blocks.

ASSEMBLING THE QUILT TOP:
All measurements have been given without seam allowance. Add ¼".

Cut the following fabrics (and add those seams!):
Background
1. Four 90° triangles, (Piece #4), 14⅛" x 14⅛" x 20". The bias should be on the 20" diagonal side.

2. Two 90° triangles, (Piece #3), 9" x 9" x 12¾". Bias should be on the two shorter sides.

3. The backing or lining piece, 54" x 42". This is larger than the quilt top; the excess can be trimmed away after the quilting has been completed.

Green borders
Four, 1" x 9", Piece #1 (add seams)
Four, 1" x 19", Piece #2 (add seams)

Red borders
Two, 1" x 43" (add seams)
Two, 1" x 30¼" (add seams)

Gray borders
Two, 4" x 51" (add seams)
Two, 4" x 38¼" (add seams)
Binding strips

Refer to the diagram at left to help with assembling the top.

1. Sew two blocks together to make Row A.

2. Sew three blocks together to make Row B.

3. Sew the remaining blocks together to make Row C. Do not sew these three rows to each other at this time.

4. Attach a 1" x 9" strip, Piece #1, onto the lower left edge of Row A, and another 1" x 9" strip onto the upper right edge of Row C.

5. Attach a 1" x 19" strip, Piece #2, along the upper edge of Row A+#1, and another to the lower edge of Row C+#1.

6. Attach the remaining Pieces #1 to the lower edge of one triangle, Piece #3, and to the upper edge of the other triangle, Piece #3.

7. Attach these triangle units, composed of Pieces #3+#1 to the ends of Row A+#1, and to Row C+#1.

8. Attach the remaining strips, Pieces #2 onto the ends of Row B. Stop sewing about three inches from the lower left edge on one side and about three inches from the upper right edge on the other side, (shown by x's on the illustration above left).

9. Sew the assembled Row A to Row B, and sew the assembled Row C to Row B.

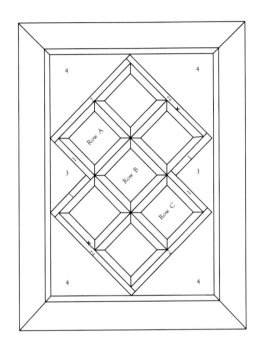

Diagram for assembling the top.

10. Finish attaching the strips started in step 8.

11. Attach the four corner triangles (Piece #4). Press.

12. Attach the narrow red borders and the four outer 4" borders using your usual methods. Prepare the quilt top for quilting.

MARKING THE CENTER FOR QUILTING:

The quilting in the center rectangle of the quilt is shown in the color photograph, above right. The quilting in the seven appliqued blocks is quite basic. There is some quilting in the leaves and petals and in the flower center. The applique is outline quilted.

The dogwood flower was also used as the inspiration for the quilting design in the four triangular corners of the quilt. Make stencils in template plastic using the two patterns on pages 55 and 56. You will need to drill holes or cut channels into them using the technique described in Chapter Five. Center the large dogwood stencil in the corner triangle so the side without the leaf faces the green border. Trace the outline and mark the dots or channels. Position the smaller template in the lower corners and trace. The background fabric will be quilted ¼" from all seams so you may want to draw these lines also.

The two triangles on the sides of the quilt were simply quilted in a series of decreasing triangles. The first lines were drawn ¼" in from the borders. The second lines were drawn 1" in from those. Finally, a third set of lines were drawn 1" in from the second lines to finish the design.

MARKING THE BORDERS FOR QUILTING:

There were several decorative borders on the library building that could have been adapted for the border quilting pattern. Slides were taken of each of the borders. Sometimes structural barriers, locations of the embellishment or some other obstacles can make it difficult or even impossible to get directly in front of your subject to obtain an accurate photograph or slide. This was the case with this terra cotta border. As mentioned before, it was located about nine feet above ground level. A slide was taken with a telephoto lens from across the street. Even though I had a good quality slide, there was some distortion. I could not trace the projected image exactly as it appeared on the paper taped to the wall. However, I was able to figure out a way to trace part of it so that it could be used to make the quilting design for the border.

One-half of the circle and scroll were drawn from the image

ABOVE: *A detail of the quilting in the flower, corner and border.*
Photo: Benkert Photography.

BELOW: *One-half of the terra cotta design was traced from the projected slide, and then flipped to reverse the pattern.*

projected by the slide. Then this section was traced onto a sheet of tracing paper and flipped upside down to reverse the drawing, as shown left. It was lined up with the first drawing and traced again to make a complete pattern unit. Continuing to use this technique, I was able to make my stencil as long as I wanted it to be for my border quilting.

1. Mark the outer border ¼" from the seam line.

2. Make a quilting stencil in template plastic using the three pattern segments below and on page 57.

3. Place the stencil in the left corner, centering it within the edges of the border. Refer to the photograph on page 54 for placement.

4. Trace the outline, working toward the middle of the border and moving the stencil as needed.

5. Repeat steps three and four, working from the right corner toward the center.

6. You will notice that the two circles at the end of the stencil will overlap or connect on the end borders, whereas they will butt against each other on the side borders.

7. After all of the marking has been completed, prepare the backing, batt, and top for quilting.

8. When the quilting has been completed, bind the outer edges with fabric to match the border.

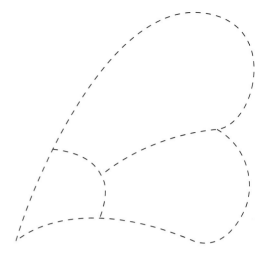

Smaller template pattern for corner triangles.

{ B } in stencil patterns indicates an area where a "bridge" is left between the sides of the stencil to strengthen it.

Left Segment

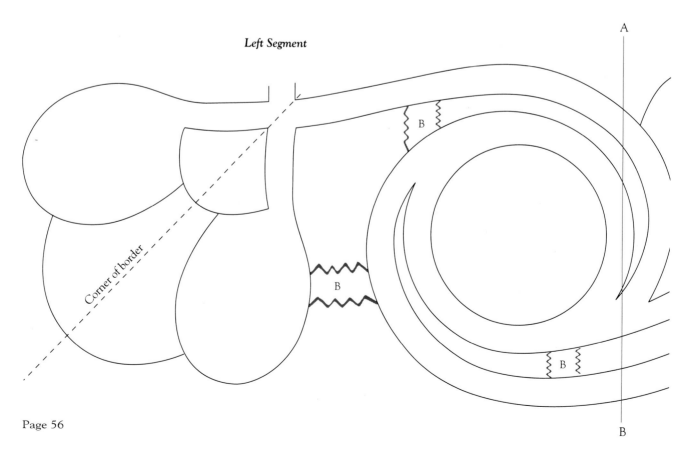

Corner of border

A

C

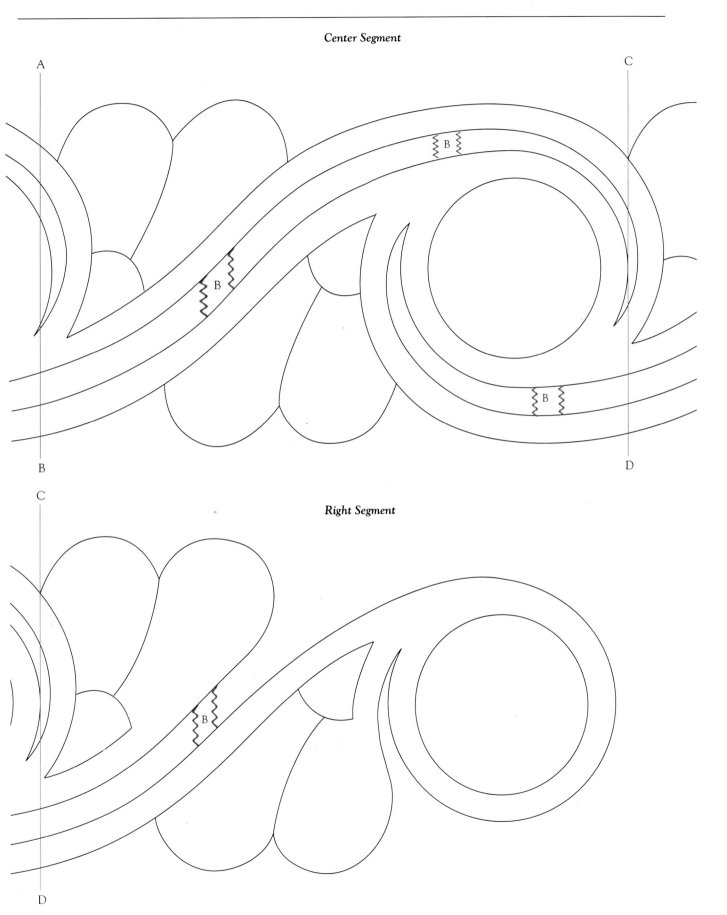

B

B

B

B

D

C

Right Segment

B

D

8
CHAPTER

FLOWER GARDEN BORDER

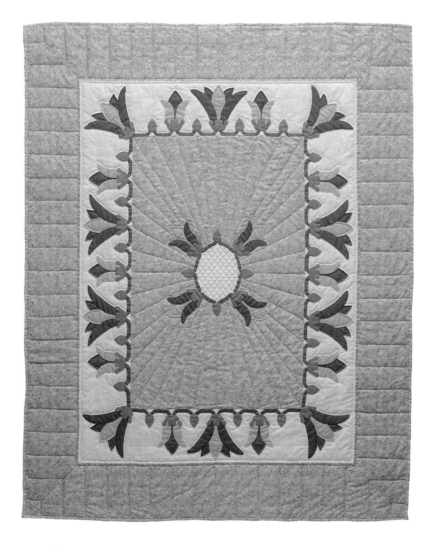

LEFT: *FLOWER GARDEN BORDER, 44″ x 54″, designed and made by the author, 1990. Photo: Benkert Photography.*

BELOW: *Double row of terra cotta frieze separated by bricks.*

The first time I saw this decorative trim on the front of an old vacant store, I knew it could be used as a pattern for a quilt. It would be necessary, though, to adapt the terra cotta design to make it suitable for textiles. Sharp petal points and tiny curves are easy to execute in clay, but difficult to duplicate with appliqued fabric.

After analyzing the photographs I had taken of the window and door trim, I decided to use the flower with five petals from one border and the bud shape from the other border. I changed the double calyx base into a single one, and the shape between the flowers and buds became a leaf.

My next decision was to determine the dimensions of the quilt so that it would not be too difficult to calculate the spacing between the buds, leaves, and flowers. After a little trial and error, I settled on a 20" x 30" center rectangle with 12" borders. That would allow exactly 2½" between the pieces of applique work, and the first leaf would start 2½" from the corner.

The drawings were done freehand on a sheet of paper that I had folded in half. The sharp tips on the petals and buds were rounded to make them easier pieces to applique. I decided to shape these small applique pieces using spray starch and cardboard templates. I also decided to make two large silhouette templates out of template plastic. One would be used to mark the applique on my center medallion and the other would be used to mark the four borders. This would be a quick and accurate way to position the applique pieces.

SUPPLIES:

4 yds. fabric for background, borders, and binding
⅝ yd. blue solid (Borders C & D)
⅜ yd. pink solid (Borders E & F, oval B)
⅜ yd. medium blue solid
⅜ yd. medium rose solid
⅛ yd. medium green solid
⅛ yd. light green solid
Thread to match applique fabrics
Marking pencil
Yardstick
Template plastic
Basic sewing equipment
Crib-size batt, 45" x 60"
Quilting thread

MEDALLION CENTER:
Measurements have been given without seam allowances. Add ¼".

1. Cut a 20" x 30" rectangle, A, out of background fabric. Remember, add seam allowances.

2. Cut out the medallion oval, pattern below, in pink fabric. *Do not* add a seam allowance to this piece. It will *not* be appliqued into place. The raw edges of this oval will be covered with the stems.

3. Make your applique templates from the patterns on page 61.

4. Center the oval on the rectangle. Using small running stitches along the edge, sew it in place. These stitches will be covered by the stems.

5. Cut out eight medium green stems and four light green leaves.

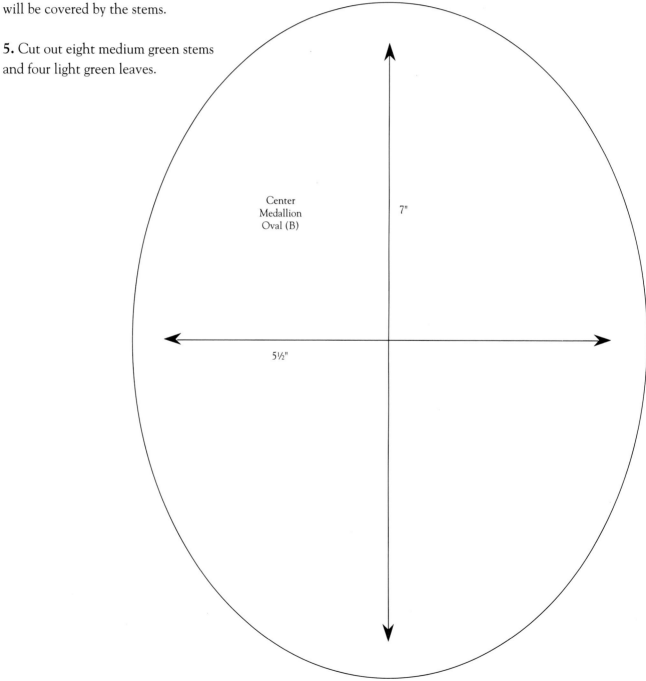

Center
Medallion
Oval (B)

7"

5½"

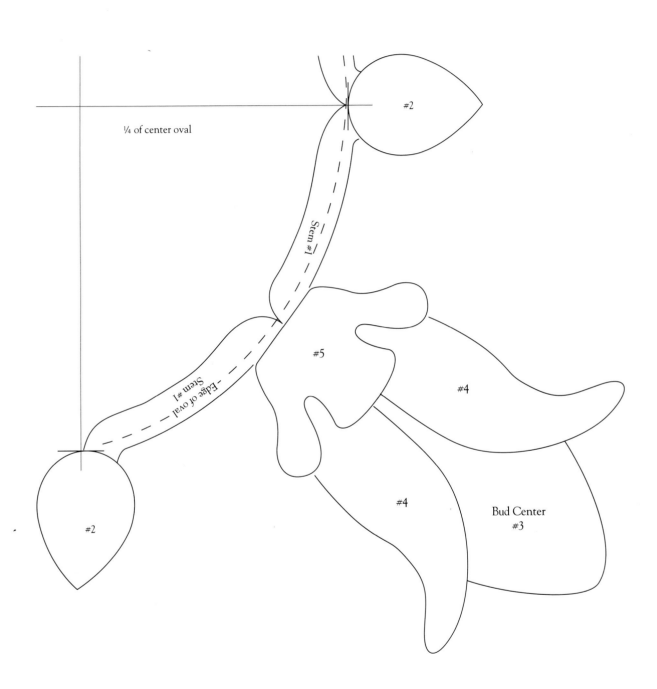

¼ of center oval

#2

Stem #1

#5

Edge of oval
Stem #1

#2

#4

#4

Bud Center
#3

6. Make a silhouette template of the stem-leaf-bud pattern, page 61.

7. Place the silhouette template on the oval so that the stems will cover the raw edges of the oval. Draw around the template to mark the outline on the oval and on the background fabric.

8. Applique the stems in place.

9. Cut the following applique pieces from your fabrics:
   8 blue outer bud petals
   4 rose inner buds
   4 light green calyxes

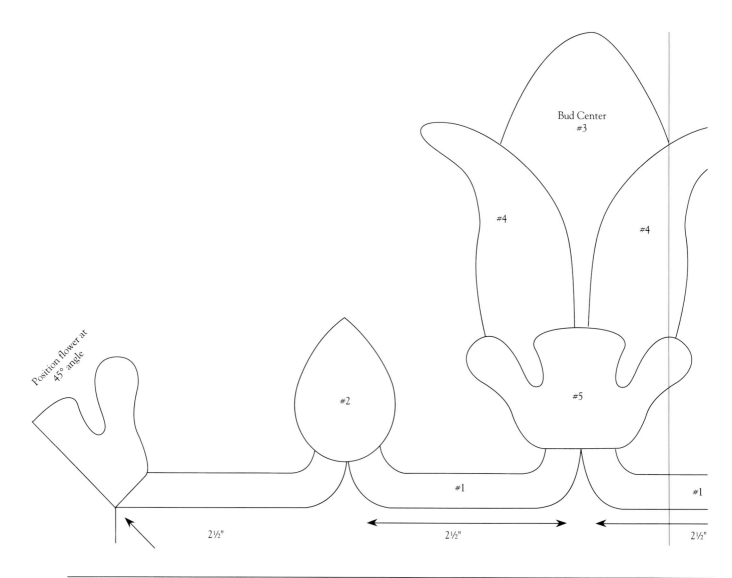

10. Line them up on your outline and applique them into place. Applique in numerical sequence given on the pattern on page 61.

BORDERS:

1. Cut two borders C, 4" x 28"; and two borders D, 4" x 38". Remember those seams.

2. Cut two borders E, 2" x 32"; and two borders F, 2" x 42", plus seams.

3. From the background fabric, cut the outer borders G, 6" x 44"; and H, 6" x 54", plus seams!

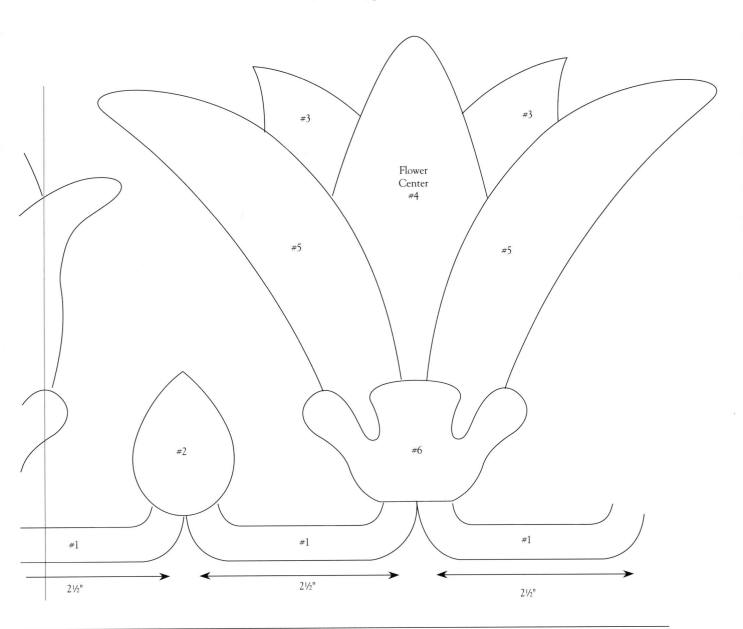

4. Assemble and attach the borders using your usual method. Miter the corners.

5. The backing or lining can also be cut out of background fabric at this time. It should be a little larger than the quilt top, about 45" x 55". The excess can be trimmed when all quilting is done.

BORDER APPLIQUE:

1. Make a silhouette template of the border pattern on pages 62 and 63.

2. Position the template along the edge of border D so that the first leaf is 2½" from the left corner. Trace lightly around the edge of the template. Refer to the diagram, page 65, for placement.

Guide for the applique placement and the quilting pattern.

3. Reverse the template to make a mirror image, and place it in the right corner. Trace the outline. There are 2½" between the calyx and the leaf.

4. Move the template to the left and line it up with the outline of the two middle leaves. Trace the outline of the middle bud.

5. Repeat these steps on the other 38" border.

6. Borders C are marked similarly. The first leaf is 2½" from the corner. Position the template in the left corner and trace the outline of the leaves, one bud, and the flower.

7. Reverse the template previously described and trace the remaining leaves and bud.

8. Make the applique templates for the stems and flowers from the border pattern, on page 63. You already have the bud and leaf templates that you used in the center medallion.

9. Cut out the following applique pieces from your fabrics:
 20 light green leaves
 32 medium green stems
 8 medium green corner stems
 20 light green calyxes
For flowers:
 20 blue outer petals

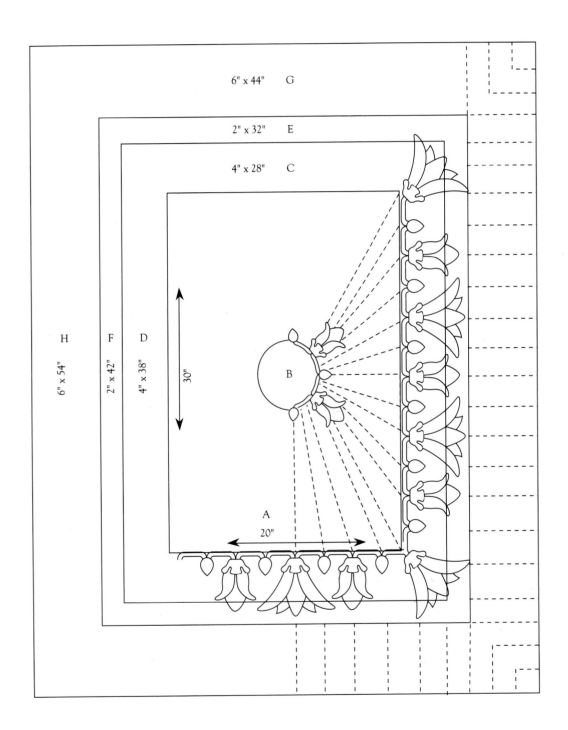

6" x 44"   G

2" x 32"   E

4" x 28"   C

H   F   D

6" x 54"   2" x 42"   4" x 38"

30"

B

A

20"

20 small blue petals
10 rose inner petals
For buds:
20 rose outer bud petals
10 blue inner buds

10. Refer to the diagram, page 65, for placement. Line up the stems along the outline on your borders and applique.

11. Line up the leaves with the outline and applique in place.

12. Line up the flower and bud pieces with the outline and applique into place according to the numerical sequence shown on the patterns. When all of the applique is completed, prepare the piece for quilting.

QUILTING:

The center oval is quilted in a diagonal or diamond grid. A diagonal line was drawn from the base of the upper left calyx to the base of the lower right calyx. This was repeated with the remaining two calyxes. Additional diagonal lines were drawn ½" apart in each direction to make the grid.

The selection of your background fabric may influence your quilting designs. I chose a print for the quilt shown, so an intricate quilt design would not have been very noticeable. The design created by the stitching would have been lost against the floral pattern. Therefore, I decided to quilt simple straight lines in the background and outline the outer edges of the applique. Please use the photograph below as a guide.

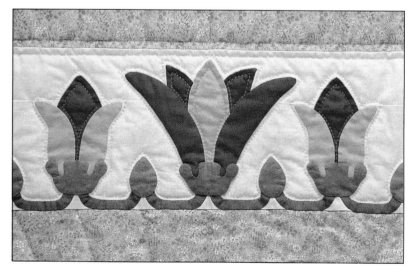

LEFT: *Outline quilting was done around the outer edges of the applique. Straight lines were quilted in the outer border. Photo: Benkert Photography.*

1. Find the center inside the oval and mark it with a pin. All of the quilting within the 20" x 30" rectangle, B, will radiate from this point.

2. Place one end of a yardstick on the pin, and line it up with the flower calyx on border D. Draw a stitching line from the edge of the oval to the bottom of the calyx, between the stems.

3. Rotate the yardstick to connect the yardstick from your pin to the bottom of the leaves and to the calyxes on all of the borders.

4. Borders C/D and E/F do not have very much quilting, only outline quilting around the edges of the applique. Additional quilting is optional.

5. Borders G and H are quilted in straight lines, 2½" apart. The tips of the buds, flowers, and leaves can be used as the guidelines for drawing quilting lines.

6. When the quilting has been completed, bind the edges with a fabric that matches the outer border.

FRIENDSHIP CIRCLE

The extraordinary mosaic tile floor shown on page 69 was found in the small foyer of an old building. The building entrance was sandwiched between shop windows and the doors of adjacent businesses; it was only by chance that I happened to glance inside. The foyer was narrow and poorly lit, and there was a stairway running into it. These conditions made it impossible to photograph the floor without some distortion. There was no way to obtain a direct camera angle, short of being suspended in mid-air; any patterns would have to be drawn freehand from photographs. But I knew that I wanted to use this floor design for a wallhanging.

LEFT: *FRIENDSHIP CIRCLE, 40" x 40", designed and appliqued by the author, 1990, hand quilted by Anita Murphy, Kountze, Texas. Photo: Benkert Photography.*

ABOVE: *The mosaic tile floor shown above was the inspiration for FRIENDSHIP CIRCLE. A photograph was taken, enlarged, and used as the guide for the freehand drawing.*

I decided to omit the interlocking circles because I only wanted to make one of the floral patterns; even though I realized that the entire floor pattern would make an exceptional bed quilt. I also decided to eliminate the small center circle in the design because I thought it looked like a target. The ribbons and swags of leaves and flowers were simplified to make them easier to applique. Even enlarged, the leaves were still quite small and narrow at the base. I liked the colors of the tiles, so I decided not to change them when I selected my fabrics.

I decided to use a circle with a 24" diameter. I drew it on a large sheet of paper, divided it into eight equal sections, like pie wedges, and made the drawing within one of those sections. I traced it on tracing paper to get the mirror image for the second section. The drawing shown above resulted. My templates were made from this drawing.

SUPPLIES:
2 ¾ yd. background fabric
1 ⅛ yd. rose solid for borders and binding
1 yd. blue solid for borders
⅛ yd. dark salmon solid for flowers
⅛ yd. peach solid for flowers
⅛ yd. each, light, medium, and dark green solids
⅛ yd. each, light and medium blue solids for ribbons
Thread to match applique
White basting thread

Marking pencil
Batting, 40" x 40"
Basic sewing supplies
Sheet of Manila tagboard or poster board, 27" square
Template plastic
Quilting thread
Yardstick and compass attachments

CONSTRUCTING THE TOP:
All measurements are given without seam allowances. Add ¼".

1. From your background fabric, cut a 27" square for the quilt top and a 42" square for the backing or lining. Remember, you must add seam allowances.

2. Cut all of the border pieces: four blue strips 1" x 29", four rose strips ½" x 30", four background borders 5" x 40". Seams should be added. Refer to the color photograph at the beginning of the chapter for placement of these borders.

3. Assemble and attach the borders to the 27" square of background fabric using your usual methods. Miter the corners. The circular borders are rings of fabric which are appliqued onto the 27" background square. They do not have any seams. Making Manila tagboard or poster board templates will simplify marking the narrow borders on the rose and blue fabrics. It is difficult to draw such large narrow circles directly on fabrics using a yardstick with compass attachments because the fabric tends to slip and bunch under the pencil tip.

4. Make templates of these two rings. They can both be made from the same sheet of tagboard or poster board. The inner ring is ½" wide. It has an inside diameter of 24", and the outside diameter is 25". The second ring is 1" wide. It has an inside diameter of 25" with an outside diameter of 27".

5. Tape the fabric for the larger ring to a smooth surface with masking tape to prevent it from slipping. Tape the 1" wide cardboard template on the fabric using four or five little pieces of masking tape. Trace around the inner and outer edges of this template using your favorite marking tool.

6. Repeat step five with the ½" ring, but remember to allow extra for seams or the "tuck under" before you cut out these big rings.

7. I suggest that you baste the fabric rings to your background square prior to appliqueing them into place. They are large, narrow, and floppy, and they have lots of bias which could stretch out of shape.

8. Applique only the outer edge of the 1" ring. The inside raw edges will be covered by the second ring of fabric.

9. Baste the ½" ring in place, covering the raw edge of the first ring. Applique both edges of this second ring. After completing these applique steps, applique the flower garlands and ribbons.

MARKING THE APPLIQUE PATTERN:
1. Make a silhouette template of the flower swag and ribbon by tracing only the outline of the applique pattern (page 72) on template plastic. The template will look similar to a comet because it will have a flower at only one end! It should look like the silhouette template shown left.

2. Divide the circular section of the quilt top into quarter sections and mark them.

3. Place the lower edge of the flower petal on the silhouette template ¾" from the inside edge of the narrow appliqued ring. Be sure that the flower is centered over one of the quarter division marks on the circle. The tip of the outer swag leaf should be 5¾" from the outer edge of that ring. Refer to the diagram on page 73. Trace lightly around your template.

4. Proceed to the next mark. Reverse the template to get a mirror image of the first swag. Measure carefully, just as you did in step three. Trace. Repeat these steps in the remaining three sections of the circle.

5. Do not trace the flower that is closest to the center of the circle. It can be easily appliqued into place after all of the other applique work has been completed. Some of these petals will partially cover the edges of some of the leaves at the end of the swag.

This silhouette template was used to mark the position of the applique pieces.

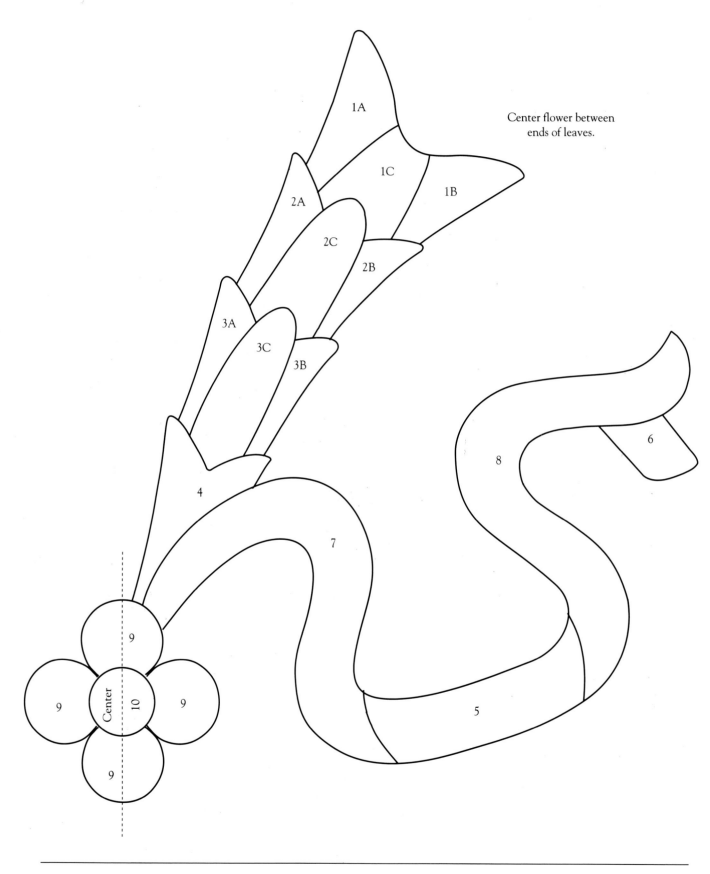

Center flower between
ends of leaves.

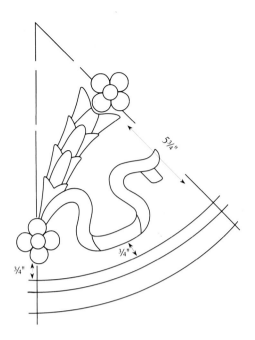

ABOVE: *Placement guide for applique. This is one-eighth of the pattern.*

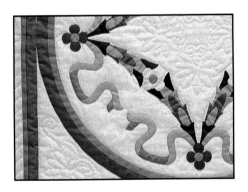

ABOVE: *This is a detail of the quilting around the swags and center of the quilt. Photo: Benkert Photography.*

APPLIQUE:

1. Make your applique templates from the pattern on page 72.

2. Cut out the fabric applique pieces. Refer to the photograph below for color placement. Notice that the sides of the leaves are quite narrow and taper sharply. I suggest that you allow a wider than normal seam on the inside edges of the three pairs of leaves, 1A and 1B, 2A and 2B, and 3A and 3B. These pieces will be easier to applique if there is a little more fabric to hold. After each pair of leaves has been appliqued in place, trim back the excess seam allowance. Leaves 1C, 2C, and 3C can then be appliqued in place over these edges.

3. Applique in the numerical sequence given on the pattern, starting with piece 1A. After the four edge flowers, and all of the swags and ribbons have been stitched into place, applique the flowers between the ends of the swags. Use pieces 9 and 10 for these flowers.

MARKING THE QUILT DESIGN:

The patterns for the quilting designs were adapted from a stone embellishment I found on a building in another city. The detail shown left indicates how the quilting was done around the swags, and how the quilting was done within the center of the circle.

1. Make both of the quilting patterns using template plastic. The patterns are provided on page 74. Include the center marks on your stencil because they will assist you in positioning the stencils for marking. One of the patterns will be used in the center of the circle and the border, and the other has been designed to fit into the four corners, just outside of the applique circles.

2. Place the quilting stencil between the sides of the swags so the center mark on the base of the stencil is about 1¼" from the middle of the circle. Trace the outline onto the background fabric. Repeat this step three more times, rotating the stencil a quarter turn each time.

3. Mark the background ¼" from the edges of the applique and circular border. This will outline the flowers, swags, ribbons, and inner border.

4. To mark the corners, place the quilting stencil, B, into the corner between the appliqued circle and the corner. Trace it onto the

Pattern for center and border stencil.

A

Center

Pattern for corner stencil.

B

Center

background fabric. Mark ¼" on the background fabric to outline the corner.

5. Repeat steps two to four in the remaining three corners.

MARKING THE BORDER QUILT DESIGN:

1. Find the halfway point on the border. This should be 20" from the corner. Mark this place.

2. Use the stencil that you previously used to mark the center of the quilt top, and place it ¼" from the edge of the narrow ½" border. Center it over your mark, and trace lightly around it. Repeat this on the remaining three borders.

3. The remainder of this border will be quilted in straight lines placed at a 45 degree angle. Mark the inner and outer edges on the border at 1" intervals. Work toward the stencil outline that you traced in step two.

4. Draw lines at a 45 degree angle to connect the dots. Draw from the upper left to the lower right on the right-hand side of the stencil outline, and from the upper right to the lower left on the left-hand side. Work toward the stencil outline as shown below.

5. Continue connecting the marks until you reach your stencil outline. Do not draw any lines through it.

6. Repeat steps four and five on the remaining three borders.

7. After all of the marking has been completed, prepare the quilt top for quilting.

8. When all of the quilting has been completed, bind the edges with the rose fabric.

RIGHT: *The stencil is centered on the border. Straight lines are quilted at a 45 degree angle on either side of it.*

SECTION IV

DESIGN
YOUR OWN
QUILT PATTERN

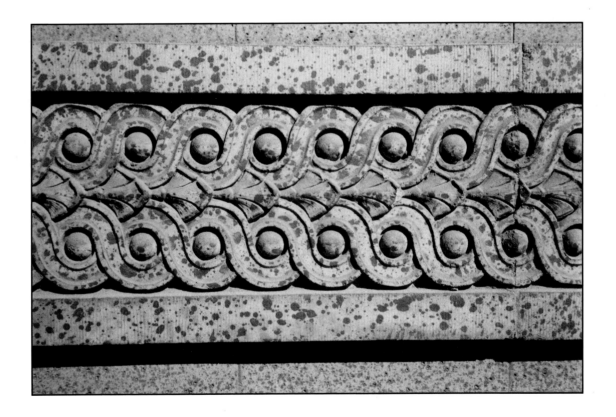

DESIGN
YOUR OWN
QUILT PATTERN

ABOVE: *Basptismal font, St. Luke's Catholic Church, St. Paul, MN.*

BELOW: *Building entrance trim, Milwaukee, WI.*

Now you are ready to try designing your own quilt pattern. You may already have an architectural embellishment that you would like to use, or perhaps you need some new ideas for a quilt pattern. Maybe you started a quilt a few months ago, but you are still looking for a special design to quilt in the plain blocks or the borders. The photographs on the following pages may provide you with just the inspiration needed to get started or to solve a design problem. The architectural embellishments in these photographs can be adapted for both blocks and border patterns.

Not all of these photographs are direct views of the decorative architectural pieces. It was frequently necessary to hang over balconies, lie on floors, balance on bannisters, or work around some other obstacle to obtain the photograph of a special piece of building ornamentation. I hope that you will be able to use these photographs of inspirational details without great inconvenience.

Two grid patterns are also included, on pages 82 and 83, so that you can have them photocopied on transparent plastic. Grab a pencil and some paper, and then let your imagination go to work!

ABOVE: *Carved newel post, Milwaukee County Historical Society, Milwaukee, WI.*

BELOW: *Carved marble fireplace, Wisconsin Memorial Park, Brookfield, WI. Photo: Violette Jahnke.*

LEFT: *Entrance detailing, Franklin Avenue Public Library, Minneapolis, MN.*

BELOW RIGHT: *Terra cotta frieze, Franklin Public Library, Minneapolis, MN.*

BOTTOM: *Terra cotta frieze, Minneapolis, MN.*

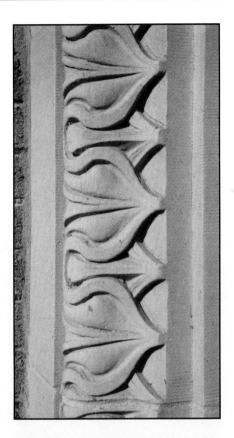

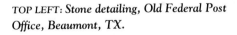

TOP LEFT: *Stone detailing, Old Federal Post Office, Beaumont, TX.*

TOP RIGHT: *Trim around windows, Franklin Avenue Public Library, Minneapolis, MN.*

ABOVE LEFT: *Interior, Cathedral of St. Paul, St. Paul, MN.*

RIGHT: *Entrance detailing, St. Luke's Catholic Church, St. Paul, MN.*

½" GRID

SUGGESTED READING

Identifying American Architecture, A Pictorial Guide to Styles and Terms: 1600-1945, by John J. G. Blumenson, published by American Association for State and Local History.

Victorious Victorians, A Guide to the Major Architectural Styles, text by Peg B. Sinclair, published by Holt Rinehart Winston, 1985.

Painted Ladies, San Francisco's Resplendent Victorians, by Elizabeth Pomada and Michael Larson, published by E.P. Dutton, 1978.

Daughters of Painted Ladies, America's Resplendent Victorians, by Elizabeth and Michael Larson, published by E.P. Dutton, 1987.

CAROL WAGNER

ABOUT THE AUTHOR

Carol Wagner is a native of the Midwest. She was born in Milwaukee, Wisconsin, where she later earned her degree in art education from the University of Wisconsin-Milwaukee.

Carol made her first quilt in 1974, "as an attempt to use up the years of accumulated scraps I had saved from sewing." That very first quilt proved to be the start of her fascination with quilting and its numerous possibilities as a means of artistic expression.

She started to teach quilt classes in her community in the early 1980's, and later became a National Quilting Association certified teacher. She now teaches and lectures to guilds across the United States, and has taught at the Quilt Festival in Houston, Texas. Carol does some free-lance writing and designing for quilt magazines and needlework books. Her articles have appeared in *Quilting Today, Quilt World, Quilter's Newsletter Magazine* and *American Quilter*.

Her quilts have received awards in local and national shows and competitions. In 1986, Carol's quilt, FREEDOM TO DREAM, was selected as the winning entry from Minnesota at the Great American Quilt Festival, the nationwide competition celebrating the Statue of Liberty's 100th birthday.

Carol, her husband, Howard, and their two children moved to Minnesota in 1964, where they reside in a suburb of St. Paul.

⟡American Quilter's Society⟡

dedicated to publishing books for today's quilters

The following AQS publications are currently available:

- **American Beauties: Rose & Tulip Quilts,** Gwen Marston & Joe Cunningham, #1907: AQS, 1988, 96 pages, softbound, $14.95
- **America's Pictorial Quilts,** Caron L. Mosey, #1662: AQS, 1985, 112 pages, hardbound, $19.95
- **Applique Designs: My Mother Taught Me to Sew,** Faye Anderson, #2121: AQS, 1990, 80 pages, softbound, $12.95
- **Arkansas Quilts: Arkansas Warmth,** Arkansas Quilter's Guild, Inc., #1908: AQS, 1987, 144 pages, hardbound, $24.95
- **The Art of Hand Applique,** Laura Lee Fritz, #2122: AQS, 1990, 80 pages, softbound, $14.95
- **...Ask Helen More About Quilting Designs,** Helen Squire, #2099: AQS, 1990, 54 pages, 17 x 11, spiral-bound, $14.95
- **Award-Winning Quilts & Their Makers: The Best of AQS Shows – 1985-1987,** edited by Victoria Faoro, #2207: AQS, 1991, 232 pages, soft bound, $19.95
- **Classic Basket Quilts,** Elizabeth Porter & Marianne Fons, #2208: AQS, 1991, 128 pages, softbound, $16.95
- **A Collection of Favorite Quilts,** Judy Florence, #2119 AQS, 1990, 136 pages, softbound, $18.95
- **Dear Helen, Can You Tell Me?...all about quilting designs,** Helen Squire, #1820: AQS, 1987, 56 pages, 17 x 11, spiral-bound, $12.95
- **Dyeing & Overdyeing of Cotton Fabrics,** Judy Mercer Tescher, #2030: AQS, 1990, 54 pages, softbound, $9.95
- **Flavor Quilts for Kids to Make: Complete Instructions for Teaching Children to Dye, Decorate & Sew Quilts,** Jennifer Amor #2356, AQS, 1991, 120 pages., softbound, $12.95
- **Fun & Fancy Machine Quiltmaking,** Lois Smith, #1982: AQS, 1989, 144 pages, softbound, $19.95
- **Gallery of American Quilts: 1849-1988,** #1938: AQS, 1988, 128 pages, softbound, $19.95
- **Gallery of American Quilts 1860-1989: Book II,** #2129: AQS, 1990, 128 pages, softbound, $19.95
- **The Grand Finale: A Quilter's Guide to Finishing Projects,** Linda Denner, #1924: AQS, 1988, 96 pages, softbound, $14.95
- **Heirloom Miniatures,** Tina M. Gravatt, #2097: AQS, 1990, 64 pages, softbound, $9.95
- **Home Study Course in Quiltmaking,** Jeannie M. Spears, #2031: AQS, 1990, 240 pages, softbound, $19.95
- **Infinite Stars,** Gayle Bong, #2283: AQS, 1992, 72 pages, softbound, $12.95
- **The Ins and Outs: Perfecting the Quilting Stitch,** Patricia J. Morris, #2120: AQS, 1990, 96 pages, softbound, $9.95
- **Irish Chain Quilts: A Workbook of Irish Chains & Related Patterns,** Joyce B. Peaden, #1906: AQS, 1988, 96 pages, softbound, $14.95
- **Marbling Fabrics for Quilts: A Guide for Learning & Teaching,** Kathy Fawcett & Carol Shoaf, #2206: AQS, 1991, 72 pages, softbound, $12.95
- **Missouri Heritage Quilts,** Bettina Havig, #1718: AQS, 1986, 104 pages, softbound, $14.95
- **Nancy Crow: Quilts and Influences,** Nancy Crow, #1981: AQS, 1990, 256 pages, hardcover, $29.95
- **No Dragons on My Quilt,** Jean Ray Laury with Ritva Laury & Lizabeth Laury, #2153: AQS, 1990, 52 pages, hardcover, $12.95
- **Oklahoma Heritage Quilts,** Oklahoma Quilt Heritage Project #2032: AQS, 1990, 144 pages, softbound, $19.95
- **Quiltmaker's Guide: Basics & Beyond,** Carol Doak, #2284: AQS, 1992, 208 pages, softbound $19.95
- **QUILTS: The Permanent Collection – MAQS,** #2257: AQS, 1991, 100 pages, 10 x 6½, softbound, $9.95
- **Scarlet Ribbons: American Indian Technique for Today's Quilters,** Helen Kelley, #1819: AQS, 1987, 104 pages, softbound, $15.95
- **Sets & Borders,** Gwen Marston & Joe Cunningham, #1821: AQS, 1987, 104 pages, softbound, $14.95
- **Somewhere in Between: Quilts and Quilters of Illinois,** Rita Barrow Barber, #1790: AQS, 1986, 78 pages, softbound, $14.95
- **Stenciled Quilts for Christmas,** Marie Monteith Sturmer, #2098: AQS, 1990, 104 pages, softbound, $14.95
- **Texas Quilts – Texas Treasures,** Texas Heritage Quilt Society, #1760: AQS, 1986, 160 pages, hardbound, $24.95
- **A Treasury of Quilting Designs,** Linda Goodmon Emery, #2029: AQS, 1990, 80 pages, 14 x 11, spiral-bound, $14.95
- **Wonderful Wearables: A Celebration of Creative Clothing,** Virginia Avery, #2286: AQS, 1991, 168 pages, softbound, $24.95

These books can be found in local bookstores and quilt shops. If you are unable to locate a title in your area, you can order by mail from AQS, P.O. Box 3290, Paducah, KY 42002-3290. Please add $1 for the first book and 40¢ for each additional one to cover postage and handling.